APPALACHIAN HERITAGE

VOL. 43, NO. 3
SUMMER 2015

ESTABLISHED IN 1973

PUBLISHED QUARTERLY
by Berea College
CPO 2166
205 N. Main Street
Berea, KY, 40404

www.appalachianheritage.net

The short stories in this publication are works of fiction. Names, characters, places, and incidents are either the products of the authors' imaginations or are used fictitiously. Any resemblance to actual events, locales, or persons, living or dead, is entirely coincidental. The views expressed in the creative nonfiction herein are solely those of the authors.

Electronic submissions only at www.appalachianheritage.net

Distributed by the University of North Carolina Press. Basic subscription price: $30/year for individuals, $40/year for institutions. For subscription requests and inquiries, visit the magazine's website, email uncpress_journals@unc.edu, or call 919.962.4201.

CONTENTS

EDITOR'S NOTE

JASON HOWARD

During their panel discussion titled "Voice Lessons" at the 2015 Appalachian Studies Association Conference, writers and teachers Darnell Arnoult, Karen Salyer McElmurray, Amanda Jo Runyon, and Jessie van Eerden offered their thoughts on voice in creative writing. They talked of the vital voices that have shaped their work over the years, a diverse chorus of influences including historical figures and events, personal experiences, family members, books, songs, recipes, Adrienne Rich, and many more. A major theme of their discussion was expectations—in their words, "what mountain writers 'are supposed to sound like'"—and how they have dealt with that pressure in their writing lives.

Since 1870—when, according to historian Henry D. Shapiro, both the idea and image of Appalachia as we know it began to be created by journalists and local color writers—those expectations have often veered from romanticized depictions of simple and picturesque lives amidst a rugged landscape to savage and backward portraits of violence and lawlessness. Appalachians became otherized in the process, viewed by a wide swath of Americans as the nation's counterpoint.

Literary writers in the region, though, pushed back against such confining stereotypical notions, with authors like Emma Bell Miles, James Still, Harriette Simpson Arnow, and Jim Wayne Miller producing works that offered complex—and often dark, hard-edged, and gut-wrenching—representations of the region and its people.

This tradition remains alive and well today in the writings of Lee Smith, Robert Morgan, Barbara Kingsolver, Crystal Wilkinson, Ron Rash, Lisa Alther, Silas House, Frank X Walker, Ann Pancake, Carter Sickels, Karen Salyer McElmurray, and countless others, including a host of emerging talents. These diverse voices are committed to presenting Appalachia not as a sentimentalized, nostalgic region, but as a three-dimensional, complicated place, filled with virtue and vice and everything in between. As such, the literature of contemporary Appalachia depicts a region that remains haunted by traditional themes including poverty, dislocation, sense of place, heritage, environmental industry, and a struggle between its people and the outside world. But it has also expanded to consider issues of race, gender, sex and sexuality, immigration, drugs, and mental health, in passages that are often alternately lyrical, gritty, and graphic.

In their enlightening new book *Studying Appalachian Studies: Making the Path by Walking*, scholars Chad Berry, Phillip J. Obermiller, and Shaunna L. Scott call for Appalachian studies and literature to "go beyond the established memes, tropes, and stereotypes that adhere to the region"—to present Appalachia in all of its many forms, places, and complexities.

In this issue—as in every issue—of *Appalachian Heritage*, you will find writings that do just that. Dan Leach's suspenseful story "Floods and Fires" challenges small town mindsets and questions how far a parent will go to protect their children. Jackson Connor's essay "Speaking of Lineage" contemplates the notions of toughness, ancestry, and masculinity. Pauletta Hansel's poem "Hateful" takes the Appalachian granny trope and turns it on its head while ruminating about gender roles and expectations.

Two special sections are also featured. One is a clutch of poems centered on music that I have titled "Pitch Perfect," with breathtaking work from poets including Marianne Worthington and Doug Van Gundy. The other comprises fiction and creative nonfiction from Arnoult, McElmurray, Runyon, and van Eerden, and is titled "Voice Lessons" after their panel discussion, placing their distinctive writing styles on full display.

Listen to these voices as they bear witness to the grit and tenderness of our diverse, complicated region. ■

IN MEMORIAM: JEAN RITCHIE

LOYAL JONES

I first met Jean Ritchie about seventy years ago at Brasstown, North Carolina, where I grew up and where her sisters Mae and Edna were at the John C. Campbell Folk School. Just a few years later, as a foreign-lander-soldier, I found a copy of *Singing Family of the Cumberlands* in the Army post library. It was a revelation to me. It was the first book I'd ever read whose author I personally knew—and it was about my own kind of people. A half century later, she and I served together on the Hindman Settlement School Board for about twenty years. She was also a member of the committee that originated and planned, and she frequently performed at the annual Celebration of Traditional Music at Berea College.

Jean was the most traditionally authentic artist in the Folk Revival and afterwards. She didn't just sing the ancient and marvelous songs and ballads that came down through the generations of her people, along with their genes, her performances took her audiences on profound cultural trips, with the help of husband George Pickow's photographs. These performances highlighted the positive values and aesthetics of her people. Thus, she counteracted the negative stereotypes that have shamed Appalachian people. Her Phi Beta Kappa intelligence led her also into scholarship. With her native artistry and the knowledge she acquired, she published many books and dozens of recordings. She also composed meaningful new songs about the strength and beauty of her people, but she also used her art and knowledge against the persistent problems and the environmental degradation of her homeland.

Jean Ritchie was an elegant and influential presence in our time. ■

FLOODS AND FIRES

DAN LEACH

Families will not be broken. Curse and expel them, send their children wandering, drown them in floods and fires, and old women will make songs of all these sorrows and sit on the porch and sing them on mild evenings. —*Marilynne Robinson,* Housekeeping

Hap Enders watched as Sheriff Huntley, who used to be a fat, freckled bully with coarse red hair and pale blue eyes, searched his garage for a wanted man. Huntley's hair, what little he had left of it, looked almost brown now, but his eyes were still a spiteful shade of blue. His reputation as a bully had followed him into adulthood, but in towns the size of Pinkerton, badges go a long way in the forgiveness of sins.

"Three years, Hap," the Sheriff said, rubbing the stubble that covered his jaw with a swollen knuckle. "Up to three years if I find out you're lying to me."

"Like I told you before, Sheriff," Hap said, raising two upturned palms in a gesture of innocence. "I haven't seen Frankie since this morning."

Sheriff Huntley shined his flashlight into the corner of the garage where it reflected against a motley collection of tools and two sets of golf clubs, neither of which had seen much use since Hap had stepped down as pastor of First Baptist. He used to play twice a week—once on Tuesday afternoons with his elders and again on Thursday evenings with a group of pastors from other local churches. He learned, after a conversation at a gas station with a former First Baptist member, that both groups still kept their tee times. The year the church hosted a tournament to raise money for a group of missionaries going to Romania, Hap was an eight handicap. But some time had passed since then.

"I guess we'll see," the Sheriff said and peeled back a tarp that had been draped, for no particular reason, over a lawnmower.

The Sheriff approached the only other door in the garage aside from the entrance to the house, eyed it wearily, and paused.

"What's in here," the Sheriff said, putting one hand on his holstered gun and the other on the door-knob.

"Frankie, of course," Hap said and smiled.

The Sheriff mouthed a curse and jerked the door open. When he discovered nothing more than a water heater, he clucked his tongue and cast a bitter look at Hap.

"Sheriff, can I offer you some sweet tea before you leave?"

Hap said, returning the glare. "If you give me a minute, I might be able to dig up a doughnut too."

The Sheriff made a show of clearing the phlegm in his throat and hocked a massive ball of it onto the pavement in front of Hap's boots. He punctuated this gesture by pushing the brim of his hat forward and whipping around on his heels like one of those boys from the Citadel. It was an impressive imitation given the fact that Huntley, like the rest of the Pinkerton Sheriff's Department, had attended community college.

"I'm not leaving yet," he said over his shoulder and let himself back into the house.

Sheriff Huntley was searching for a man, who, according to witnesses, drove a Gerber knife into Bill Bentley's windpipe following a dispute over eight ball. Witnesses also said that, following the stabbing, the man exited the bar, got onto his bike, and was last seen riding in the direction of his father's house. These details were conveyed to Hap somewhere between the Sheriff's initial insinuation—"Where the hell is your boy?"—and his conclusion that followed several minutes later—"I know he's here because he ain't got no place else to go."

"I'm sorry Sheriff," was all that Hap had said. "Haven't seen Frankie since this morning."

As far as that last thing, the Sheriff was right. Aside from Hap's house, Frankie had nowhere else to go. After bagging groceries at the Bi-Lo—a job that George Mullinax had given Frankie as a favor to Hap—he might ride down to Rita's to drink a lemonade and watch football, but never once in the ten or so years since high school had Frankie not come home to his father's house. He had lived there his entire life and, because of his condition, would, as far as everyone assumed, continue living there until Hap passed away or some other arrangement could be made.

Hap knew that in a town the size of Pinkerton it was more or less pointless to refer to Frankie's condition by its medical nomenclature. He had grown up in a small town himself and knew their tendency to fit the sprawling complexities of the real world into their crude perspectives and not the other way around. Hap had heard that, in some places, racism, sexism, and homophobia were teetering on the edge of extinction. In Pinkerton, though, all forms of prejudice were alive and well. Frankie had not turned five before someone—Hap never knew if it was one of Frankie's peers, or one of his own—deemed him a "half-tard." Frankie's actual condition, not that anyone in Pinkerton would know or care, was Hydrocephalus.

More than once Hap considered leaving Pinkerton. In the end, though, he always arrived at the same grim conclusion—mainly that kids are kids, and kids in any town of any size find

He had grown up in a small town himself and knew their tendency to fit the sprawling complexities of the real world into their crude perspectives and not the other way around.

cruelty a good deal more convenient than kindness. Like the time they told Frankie to drink from the bottle of bleach that a janitor had accidentally left in the second grade boys' restroom. Or the time they snuck out of a sleepover to go snipe hunting and left him in the middle of the woods. Or the time they tied one end of a rope to the handlebars of his bike and the other end to the hitch of a pickup and went forty down Devil's Lake Drive. Like any time they called him friend. When Hap considered other towns, it's true that none of them seemed especially worse than Pinkerton. But none of them seemed especially better either.

Frankie had lived his life in the crosshairs of men like Huntley. That tonight they got to use real guns to hunt him seemed about the only significant difference to Hap.

■ ■ ■

When the Sheriff had first arrived, Hap refused to let him in the house. As expected, Huntley got red in the face, made a few empty threats, and, when Hap still didn't budge, practically sprinted back to his cruiser. He barked something into his radio and twenty minutes later, two more cruisers pulled up. Five minutes after that, a third. There were five of them in all—Huntley leaning against his car, smoking a thin little cigarette, and the rest gathered around him.

Not one of them was over forty and, although Hap couldn't have recalled any names, he recognized all but one of them as boys who had grown up with Frankie. Whether it was at a swimming pool, a birthday party, or a little league game, at some point in their life, Hap had loomed over these men back before they had badges, or, for that matter, chest hairs, to brandish. Back when his very presence was a boundary that they feared and obeyed. They were, at one time, good boys.

The next time that Huntley knocked on the door, he was grinning so wide his cheeks had squashed his eyes into slits no bigger than dimes turned sideways.

"Like I told y'all before," Hap said, not even bothering open the screen door. "I'd invite you in, but I just turned on an episode of *Jeopardy* and I know you boys aren't too keen on games that involve grey matter."

"Open the door, Hap," Huntley said, his voice as smooth and steady as a radiator.

Huntley tapped the glass with his state championship football ring. The ring was gold and large and studded with stones, but apparently too small now to sit on anything but his pinky finger. Depending on who you asked, Huntley was the best tight end Pinkerton High ever had, an accolade that kept him out of a jail cell more than a few times. For four years, Huntley and his all-state offensive line drove around town, drinking in plain sight, fighting without provocation, and taking the finest girls Pinkerton High could offer into the backseats of their fathers' cars. The town forgave such youthful indiscretions. In return, the boys won football games.

It was the same year that Huntley won his ring that Frankie was pulled out of class by a guidance counselor and told that he needed to start thinking about his options. "Realistic options," she clarified. When Frankie let on that he was confused, she spelled it out for him. He could bag groceries at the Bi-Lo like Jim Harmon's boy. Or, Goodwill always needed help. Or, if he was feeling lucky, he could try Trey Anderson who drained septic tanks in Pinkerton and three other counties. She told Frankie that Trey paid salary and then explained to him what that meant.

"The important thing is that we have to be realistic," she said, once more, in case there was any confusion.

Frankie nodded. He said nothing about his dream of being a veterinarian.

Huntley kept tapping his ring against the glass, but Hap remained unfazed.

"Now I know under recent administrations our constitutional rights have diminished considerably, but surely an armed officer of the law still needs a warrant to enter a citizen's house?" Hap said and rested his forearm across the door frame.

When he did this, Hap noticed a sadistic little gleam in the Sheriff's eyes, a gleam that turned into a flare as he looked over his shoulder at the other three officers and winked.

"Y'all hear that screaming?" one of the officers said, moving towards the house.

"I hear it," another one said. "How about you, Ward? You hear that screaming?"

"I sure do," the fat one, presumably Ward, responded.

"Excuse us Hap, we're going to have to ask you to step aside while we investigate this," Huntley said, slinging open the screen door and shoving him so hard that he nearly toppled over. "We have probable cause to believe that someone in this house may be in trouble."

Hap watched as the officers split up and searched the rooms in his house. He leaned against the doorframe and listened as they tipped over tables and ripped open doors. He listened as they screamed his son's name. In the upstairs hallway, where voices travel like sirens down the stairwell, one officer whispered to another, "I know that fucking retard is in here somewhere. I can feel it."

"Hey, watch it," the other whispered back, the rebuke so sudden and strong that Hap, like the first officer, was stunned to hear it.

But then, after a measured pause, the same voice whispered: "He's not a retard, remember? Just a half-tard."

Two decades of such whispers and worse had not brought Hap any closer to mastering the one piece of advice that he had given Frankie after each new injustice. "Jesus said to turn the other cheek, so that's what we'll do," he would recite, doing his best to quell the bitterness burning in his own heart.

■ ■ ■

After exiting the garage, Huntley told Hap to open the attic. The attic, as the men learned after ascending the stairs, was at least ten degrees hotter than the other rooms in the house.

The heat, combined with the rank odor of boxed and forgotten things, imbued the space with the qualities of a tomb. Sheriff Huntley and the one other officer that had followed immediately removed their hats and wiped the sweat off their faces.

"To tell you boys the truth," Hap said, using his sleeve to dab his own face. "I haven't been up here in years."

"Check out that corner over there," Huntley grunted and shined his flashlight on a pile of boxes that all had CHURCH written in black magic marker across their sides.

"Watch out for possums," Hap said and, as if it had been his idea to come up, began rummaging through an open box labeled SARAH.

"What the hell do you think you're doing?" Huntley barked, pointing the gun at the back of Hap's head. "Keep your damn hands where I can see them."

Hap watched as the officers split up and searched the rooms in his house.

"Easy there, Sheriff," Hap said. "Just an old man looking through his dead wife's things. Thought I might as well do something while y'all waste your time up here."

Hap made a production of standing up slowly and raising his hands all the way over his head. Huntley seemed poised to make a new threat when a sound echoed through the room. It was the sound of something having moved.

"What was that?" Huntley said and moved his flashlight to the northeast corner of the attic.

"I told you," Hap said and coughed violently for several seconds. "Probably a possum."

Hap continued coughing as Huntley waved his hands to signal for silence.

“Shut your mouth or you will spend the night in jail,” Huntley said through his teeth.

“Can’t help it if I’m allergic to insulation,” Hap said and continued coughing as another sound came from the corner.

“Check out over there,” Huntley said, drawing a bead on the corner with the beam of his flashlight.

The other officer obeyed, shining his own flashlight into the spaces between the stacks of boxes and giving the occasional box a kick for good measure. Hap struggled to choke down a new series of coughs and Huntley continued sweeping his light across the room.

“What is all that shit?” Huntley said and leveled his beam at a massive pile of equipment jammed up against the western wall.

“Relics from a former life,” Hap said.

“What?” Huntley said and began coughing himself.

“Church stuff,” Hap said, enunciating each syllable slow and clear.

“What is that?” Huntley said, steadying his light on a large wooden box.

“That’s a coffin,” Hap said.

“What are you doing with a coffin?” Huntley said, sneering his lip in a way that, because of his moustache, seemed more comical than threatening.

“It’s for show,” Hap said. “Used it in a play.”

“A play?” Huntley echoed, same tone, same sneer.

“Of course,” Hap said. “We wanted to remind people that, before Jesus, they were dead in their sins.”

The other officer drew his leg back and gave the coffin’s side a violent kick. It had been built out of plywood and cracked severely under the blow. He delivered one more kick to the side and then raised his boot to stomp down and crack the thing from the top when Huntley screamed, “Stop it! Stop it!”

"Come again," Huntley muttered into the radio attached to his uniform.

A muffled voice spoke. Huntley smiled. Before the voice had stopped, Huntley waved the other officer over.

"They found the bike. It's down by the creek. Tracks too," Huntley said and tore off down the stairs, leaving Hap alone, without light, in the heat and the dark.

Each time an officer ran out the front door, the screen door slammed behind them. Hap counted four slams and then listened for a full minute before moving. He walked quickly to the coffin and knelt down so that his face almost touched the floor.

He pressed his lips against a crack in the wood and whispered, "You okay, Frankie?"

■ ■ ■

For the next three hours, Hap ran from window to window trying to keep up with the search. At times, it seemed that twenty or more men were dragging the woods around his house. At times, it seemed to be just Huntley and a few others. The hounds' whining would rise and then recede. Men barked to one way or another. Huntley used one of those bullhorns and talked to Frankie like he was hiding up a tree.

When it was well past midnight and most of the other officers had gone home, Sheriff Huntley knocked on the door.

"What can I do for you, Sheriff?" Hap said, this time swinging the door wide open as if to invite in an old friend.

"If he calls you," the Sheriff said, rubbing at the ashy bags that had built up beneath his eyes. "If he makes any attempt to contact you."

"You'll be the first to know," Hap interjected. "Believe it or not, Sheriff, the Bible ain't all about love. There's a lot about justice in there too."

Sheriff Huntley continued massaging his eyes, pressing in on the spot where his eyes met the top of his nose. He held his fingers there and, for a minute, it seemed like he was reflecting on this, considering the validity of it. Then he dropped his hands and turned his eyes, cold as ever, right on Hap.

"You don't teach the Bible in this town anymore," he said as if he was ridding bile from the back of his throat. "Not since they canned your ass."

The Sheriff spit at Hap's feet again, but it lacked the dramatic quality of the first time. He stomped off the porch and got into his car. All this Hap watched from the window. Hap also watched as the Sheriff pulled out of the driveway, pretended to drive down Highway 12, and then looped back around and parked behind some trees that he assumed obscured him from Hap's view.

Hap turned off all the lights and hurried upstairs into his bedroom. From drawn blinds, he watched Huntley watch his house. The clock on the bedside table flashed 1:16 a.m. in

"You don't teach the Bible in this town anymore," he said as if he were ridding vile from the back of his throat. "Not since they canned your ass."

crystalline blue bars. Hap steadied himself against the frame and waited.

The clock read 2:32 a.m. by the time the Sheriff's tail-lights disappeared, this time for real, down Highway 12.

Every muscle in his body ached from the standing, but he ran like he was young, tearing out of the bedroom and down the hallway, taking the stairs to the attic two at a time, and practically barreling into the boxes that, half a lifetime ago, he had stacked on top of the coffin.

"It's time," he said and, there in the dark, pretended to be strong as he watched his only son rise from the dead.

■ ■ ■

Thirty minutes before Sheriff Huntley had arrived at Hap's front door, Ernie White, who owned a farm four miles to the south of Hap's, received a call. A re-run of *Andy Griffith* was on in the background, but he wasn't watching it. Along with his wife, he working on a one thousand piece jigsaw puzzle that, when completed, displayed a dust-covered Robert E. Lee astride a grey horse. The phone rang and his wife got up to answer it and Ernie White, who had fought in two wars and come home to work his farm and raised three kids and never once in his life committed a crime, fitted a piece of Lee's saber that had eluded him for going on ten minutes, took the phone from his wife, listened to his best friend of forty plus years, ask him, through tears, to become an accessory.

Ernie interrupted, whispered so his wife couldn't hear, *I'll park it beneath the willow. Keys on the front left tire. Shotgun in the cab,* and returned to the living room just as his wife fit two pieces of blue sky together.

"What did Hap want?" she said.

"Nothing," Ernie replied. "Just wanted to see if I was planning on playing bridge tomorrow."

His wife mumbled something absentmindedly. She was busy working on Lee's boot.

■ ■ ■

Hap and Frankie stayed in the woods until they came to Ernie's place. It was nearly three miles and, because Frankie had rolled his ankle in the fight at Rita's, they walked it slowly, staying clear of the road and slipping into the brush whenever a car approached. Twice a police cruiser passed them, the thin veneer of leaf and branch their only protection. When they talked, they talked in whispers and spoke mostly about the ankle, about whether or not he could make it the rest of the way.

When they arrived at Ernie's, his lights were off and his gate was locked. They were crouched behind some oaks to the south of his house. A caravan of cumuli had parked in front of the moon for most of their trip, but they drifted away, as if on cue, exposing a moon as round and white as a bleached sand-dollar. They spotted the willow. And then, the truck. It was shining like a promise in the soft light of the early morning.

■ ■ ■

They stuck to backroads even after they crossed the Pinkerton County line. They rode without radio and whispered when they spoke. They studied the silhouette of each approaching car and exhaled only after it became clear that the car did not have a lightbar. After some time, they came to the mountain. The little plastic Jesus Ernie had stuck on the dashboard started shaking real hard when the pavement turned to gravel.

"Dad," Frankie said, stuttering like always, but hoarser than usual.

"Yeah?" he replied, turning on his brights and slowing down to take the first of two dozen turns sharp enough to send an unsuspecting driver careening over the edge.

"Where are we going?" Frankie said and pawed at his left eye which was too swollen to see out of.

When Frankie first came home, Hap had cleaned him up—not properly, but just enough so that he would not drip blood on the way to the attic. Since then, Hap had avoided looking at his face. He looked now though, only for a moment. The eye was bad, but so was the gash on his head and the deep cut across his cheek and the finger on his right hand that looked as if it had been trapped beneath a cinder block. It did not, Hap thought, look like the work of one man. But, like the other times, Frankie would not tell unless he was asked and, like the other times, Hap knew the details before Frankie ever told him. Names and faces might change, but the ongoing celebration of the strong over the weak had, more or less, been developed into a formula in Pinkerton. Their violence was as predictable as their politics and their victims were chosen with no more forethought than an alligator gives to a gazelle. "It is what it is," a friend had once counseled Hap. He accepted the counsel without question. Frankie was born into an unfair fight and Hap had no illusions about the tables ever turning.

"Leave that eye alone, son," Hap said, returning his eyes to the road. "We are going someplace safe."

"Are we going to Pa Pa's?" Frankie said.

"We are," Hap said. "But not the place you're thinking of."

Frankie's mouth hung slack as he projected his confusion onto the dashboard.

"Pa Pa built two cabins," Hap said and rubbed Frankie's shoulder. "But I never told you about the second one, did I?"

"You sure didn't!" Frankie replied and waved his finger the way that parents on television do when a child has committed some harmless act of defiance.

"Well, would you like me to tell you about it now?" Hap said.

"Yes, sir, I would," Frankie said and continued massaging the eye with his thumb.

"Okay. Well, your Pa Pa built one cabin when he was a young man. About your age, actually. And that's the cabin we stay at when we go fishing. Like the time you caught that eight pound spotted bass. You remember that?"

Frankie nodded and smiled a bloody, but wide, smile. Hap winced, noticing, for the first time, Frankie's canine, cracked clean in half.

"Well, when Pa Pa got to be about my age," Hap continued. "He built another cabin. It was much smaller than the first one and it wasn't built on a lake either. Your Pa Pa built this second cabin and didn't tell anybody about it."

"It was a secret?" Frankie said, eyes wide with wonder.

"That's right," Hap said.

"And you were the only one he told," Frankie continued. "Because he was your father and you were his son."

Hap felt the old familiar tension rising up in his chest, a tension pulled on one side by the whole truth—ugly and indigestible even for someone without Frankie's condition—and on the other by a half-truth—sweetened for consumption like a cube of sugar that soaks up a bitter dose of medicine. Sometimes it seemed you lost either one you told. Like when Frankie asked why he wasn't invited to certain birthday parties. Or when Frankie asked where his mother went. Like when he asked why Hap didn't work for the church anymore.

"Nope," Hap said, too tired to find a suitable lie. "He kept that house a secret until he killed himself, Frankie. He left me a note so that I could find his body and return it to the family plot in Pinkerton."

Hap let fragments of that memory—the gun, the chair, the boards soaked in blood—flash across his thoughts, but like always he caught them before they got too far and cleared them away with a hard blink. He did not think of his father's face.

"Oh," Frankie said and struggled to process the information. "Why did you never talk about it, Dad?"

"Because," Hap said, discovering his reason as he opened his mouth. "Things get forgotten when you don't talk about them. And some things need to be forgotten. They're better off that way. Does that make sense, son?"

Frankie nodded and they drove on through the darkness, thinking and not speaking. When, after half an hour of driving, Hap heard a wheezing sound, he looked over and found Frankie sleeping, curled up in fetal position and facing the door. Hap put both hands on the wheel to take a turn and then slowed down and looked over at Frankie. He had always slept like that—shrunken and curled up, as if braced against some impending blow.

Hap continued driving and, without intending to, thought about Huntley—where he was at that moment and in what position he slept. If Hap had to guess, he would have said on his back, loose and sprawled out, like a man who for twenty some odd years had never feared anything, never stared into the darkness and trembled.

Jesus trembled when the truck bumped over a stone and His tiny plastic head shook with a spastic rhythm that drew Hap's eye.

Why? Hap whispered to Him, the word not plucked from his head and prepared for speech, but rather slung like a stone straight from some strange corner of his heart.

And without intending to, he repeated the word three times, each time increasing in volume and intensity. Meanwhile Jesus just kept shaking His head.

I've been following You ever since I was a boy. I've seen You do the most amazing things and I've been grateful for Your grace in my life. And when I saw the bad, when I saw things so horrible that it don't seem like a loving God could ever allow them, I never asked why, did I?

When I saw all the hurt and all the brokenness and all the injustice that You let go on down here, what did I say? I said that Your thoughts were higher. I said that Your ways were better. I saw all the bad and I followed You anyway and tried my best to make You proud.

And never once have I asked You why.

Frankie flinched in the seat beside him, both hands shooting up to protect his face from whatever force had threatened him in his dreaming. Hap placed a hand on his shoulder and held it there until Frankie relaxed again.

Looking back at Jesus, Hap continued.

Well, I'm asking now.

I know it's not right of me to ask and I know I, of all people, don't deserve to hear from You. But, I'm asking because I can't go on any further not knowing why. I'm sorry Father, but faith just ain't enough anymore.

Why? If all of this could be restored. If right now You have the power to fix everything. How—I mean—why wouldn't You—

Frankie flinched in the seat beside him, both hands shooting up to protect his face from whatever force had threatened him...

Hap's mouth hung open, unable to finish the thought. He stopped trying.

You know what I'm asking.

You know my heart.

And if there's a way that You can help me. If there's a way that You could speak to me tonight. Then I need to hear from You.

Please.

Hap slowed the truck to a halt. He closed his eyes and sat in silence for several minutes, waiting, and then, just as suddenly as he had spoken the first word, he reached his arm out of the open window, his fingers outstretched as if reaching for something just beyond his grasp. He looked to the sky and waited, the soft wheeze of Frankie's breathing the only sound for miles.

It was the only sound for miles.

■ ■ ■

After a while, Hap opened his eyes. It was no longer dark outside. In the east, the tops of the trees were backlit by a pale blue glow. He looked ahead and recognized the upcoming turn as the final one before the cabin. He took it, slower than the rest, and pulled carefully into the drive. He removed the keys from the ignition and looked up at the cabin that, although he had only seen it twice in his life, took on a strangely familiar look in the morning light. He listened to birds and crickets and the wind in the trees. He smelled the air and it smelled clean and weightless.

Hap climbed out of the truck and went around to Frankie's side. He opened the door and, for a moment, watched Frankie sleep. Not wanting to wake him, Hap bent down and scooped the boy into his arms. When he straightened up, he was surprised at how light Frankie was. He turned, shutting the door with his hip, and started walking towards the cabin.

Leaves crunched beneath his feet, loud enough to stir Frankie. His one good eye opened and he said, "I'm sorry, Dad. I'm sorry for everything."

As if he were lifting a pillow, Hap brought Frankie's head to his lips and kissed him on his crown where blood had dried into his hair.

"Don't you ever apologize to me, son," Hap whispered in his ear. "You have done nothing wrong."

Frankie started, "But, Dad, I—"

"You're perfect," Hap said, setting him down on the stairs to the porch. "And that's all you've ever been."

Frankie touched his fingers to his eye and winced.

"I'll run to store a little later and get something for that," Hap said, rubbing Frankie's shoulder blades.

Hap let his hand rest on Frankie's shoulder as his mind raced to compose a list of all the things they would need. There was the food, the water, the clothes, and a dozen other things that they would need within the week. The list was staggering and, when the parameters of Huntley's search widened, a simple trip to the grocery would become an incalculable risk. For every basic need, a dozen complications became apparent. But Hap ignored them all. His mind was perfectly blank and with Frankie's head resting on his shoulder, he breathed in the morning air and watched the first of a thousand new suns spilling through the branches. ■

MEMORATE

The field. Light. Morning.
Then, my father, uncle.
Apples, everywhere.
In boxes, in palms, in teeth.
Apples, everywhere.
The black mare. Wild.
The black mare that dawned
from the mountain. Wild.
The rough sketches
of my earliest memory.
My father places me on the back
of the beast & we take off
fast, faster into memory.
I didn't—I would never do that,
My father says. *That never happened.*

CHRISTIE COLLINS

MINING FOR SAPPHIRES

One minute I'm stumbling
into a classroom with a plan
to teach narrative writing,
and the next minute
I'm edging down
the dirt pile at the mine
with two plastic pails full
of wet dirt & gravel.
My father, quilted in flannel,
waits at the bottom of the hill,
his pails teeming, hopeful.
We move to the troughs
where the mountain water
washes down in waves.
Now, I'm dipping my third
fist full of raw dirt
onto the wash screen,
placing the wash screen
into the running water.
The freckled boy & his father
next to us hit the jackpot:
a ten carat natural sapphire.
My father looks at me, astonished,
his eyes wide, new. The child in him
says to me, his child:
treasure, buried treasure.
Now, I'm running my fingers
quickly over the ruddy gravel
left on the screen. We're on
our tenth or twelfth refill
of dirt when the sun beds

somewhere behind the Blue Ridges.
The few flecks of blue we hauled,
the shiny rocks which spoke to us
deep in our blue jean pockets.

CHRISTIE COLLINS

THE ATTACK

DARNELL ARNOULT

An excerpt from The Nine Lives of Loody Tibbett, *a novel in progress*

Day 1

Iron. Sodium. Lightning. Wind. Stars.

■ ■ ■

Day 10

There's a flap and roll to it, the kind of soft thunder you hear when you hang sheets on the line and a strong wind comes while you're in the middle of it all and the sheets and pillow cases, all that slick damp cotton, slaps and whips and furls about you. Fresh cotton slides across my bare skin. It smells like sunshine but there's no color.

I believe I might have died. Am I dead?

■ ■ ■

Day 15

If this is death, it is peaceful seeming enough, but I'm disappointed. I thought the need, the yearning, would die with the body.

■ ■ ■

Day 35

It's all here, wherever I am. The songs slide and hum in the valleys and hills of this roiling cotton. I feel history as I felt it then, before it was history. I'm an old woman floating like a rock between life and death. I was once young and danced between death and life. I had hoped I could forget all that.

■ ■ ■

Day 43

My brain pops popcorn all the time now. *Pop, pop, pop,* it goes. Some firecracker kernel goes off and there's a piece of it. It can be a day, or a week, or a month—whole, fully blossomed from the heat of my brain trying to find its way. Maybe it's an hour, just an hour that comes at me hot and fast, as I sprawl here frozen. Sometimes it's more like a freight train zinging at me so hard and heavy, I think it could kill me, but I don't move, don't jump back. I can't move, goddamnit.

Pop. I'd just finished helping Mavis milk eighteen cows in two hours time. Then she put me to shucking a barrel full of corn for the hogs, shucking out the ears so the cows could have the shucks. That's how it is when you're a sharecropper's daughter. You got to use it up, even the dirt under your fingernails. You work for food if there's nothing else to work for.

Daddy hired me out after I botched the marriage to the preacher. Hank was in the Navy by then, and he sent what money he could to help out. We both tried to make it up to Daddy, but he had eight other children to feed. Even after I was married, everybody called me "Pink's oldest girl." Like that was my name, like I didn't have no name of my own. Even after I was grown, folks called me "Pink's grown girl."

■ ■ ■

Day 44

It didn't take long after Hank left for Daddy to come find me and give me to old Mavis Lupin and her husband Joe. Three of the young'uns Mama left when she died weren't big enough to work, not even to make biscuits, so it was up to me to help him keep up. If I hadn't known what a bad spot he was in, I'd have told him Joe beat me with a strop when he was drinking, finding some thing I'd done what displeased him. And then Mavis wouldn't look at me, afraid she'd get the strop next, after Joe was done with me.

Daddy wouldn't have put up with that. He never laid a hand on none of us, not a time. It was Mama that spanked if need be. But Daddy might kill Joe Lupin for laying into me with leather, and then what shape would we all be in? So I took the stripes and kept on working. Besides, it wasn't Joe I was most afraid of, and Mavis was most likely afraid of me.

Wally was the one made me wary. But you can't hardly work on a farm with no more than three other people and not find yourself alone. You got to get it done—get it done before breakfast, get it done before lunch, get it done before supper, get it done before dark, get it done before bed. You got to get the cows milked and get the corn shucked and get the beans picked and get the tomatoes skinned and in the steaming jars, and get the eggs from the nest, and hunt the laid eggs from the ones that refuse to set a nest no matter how much wire you put up. There's washing and hanging the wash and taking it down and sprinkling the clothes and balling them up and standing over a hot iron on a July day with the smell of homemade starch in your nostrils and the starch itself making your hands tacky and your back hurting so bad you can't take a good breath. If you do, the hot air just makes you want water, and your water bottle's all empty 'cause you've used it to sprinkle them clothes. And it just starts over every day, every hour of daylight. So that shucking corn behind the barn is almost like taking a break. Sitting on some upturned bucket, pulling back on the pale green husks over and over so that letting your back stretch out over your bones turns to some kind of relief. Then you forget not to be alone. You forget to listen behind you 'cause you're in the rhythm of your toil, that song your body sings getting through its hard day, getting through to the time when you can lay your head down and go away from your hard life for a few hours, rest a little while 'til that goddamn rooster crows and pulls you back into it while you kick and scream in your dreams to stay asleep.

Pop. Pop. Just let me sleep. If I don't never find my way, I'll turn to dust remembering what work is. Just let me sleep.

■ ■ ■

Day 50

My mind's hot, grease-hot. I can pop sacks and sacks of corn. But my body's cold and limp as a dead fish, a stacked stone pulled from the field, a thirsty pillar. There was a time my body moved like something born to the fire of motion. I never was one to sit still till I was bone tired. Hell, even my feet kept moving in my sleep, foot over foot over foot, sliding and pushing. Now only my mind can rush forward and run back.

■ ■ ■

Day 62

Now that I know I'm alive, I have spells of wishing I'm not. Sometimes I dream I'm already in the grave. The dark opens over me and I hear Hub slide the last rock in place. Then I burst into a cloud of tiny lights. And the lights rise up through the earth, through Hub who covers me like a quilt, through the air of the blue sky, until black space with no lights at all, where I must have started. The darkness opens again and again and again and again.

■ ■ ■

Day 90

Only my finger hops a little, like a frog when it knows it's being watched and it's trying to sneak away, but my finger always hops too late and nobody knows.

■ ■ ■

Day 111

They ask me over and over what my name is, like I didn't hear them the first time. I've got too many names in my head, too many to choose from, and I don't know what to say, and if I did, I couldn't speak it. I can't hold onto any names long enough to put something in order. Nothing's in order. Just *pop, pop, pop*. Corn clouds scatter about the hot skillet. Sometimes the pops wake me up. They are so short and angry, they'd make me jump if I could jump.

While I peeled back on one of those papery husks, Buck come up behind me, grabbed me just below my shoulders, pulled me up with my arms pinned under his, and then he threw me down in the dirt behind the barn. I tucked my chin into my chest to keep from hitting my head on the ground. All the same, my face slid in the brown pebbled slick that smelled of cow piss.

■ ■ ■

Day 112

Just let me sleep. I'm hit by another freight train. Just let me sleep, goddamnit.

■ ■ ■

Day 114

I see light on one side. Shadows shift. My eyes must be open.

■ ■ ■

Day 115

"Loody, can you say 'Loody'?"

He's staring at me, talking too loud and staring at me with his big brown eyes wide and a smile on his face as fake as a plastic duck's. "Come on, try. L-l-l-l-l-l-o-o-o-o-o-d-d-d-d-e-e-e. Make the L sound—l-l-l-l-l-u-u-u-u-l-l-l-l." I want to ask him who he is, but my mouth's like a wet dish rag. It won't stand up to my words, won't take a shape. "L-l-l-l-l-o-o-o-o-o-d-d-e-e-e," he says. I know his face.

I pluck the name from his mouth and throw it in the skillet. It pops and skidders away like the rest. They're swirling around my head like lights at a fair, the names. But I can't reach up and grab a one of them, not even the one he called. Then it comes to me who he is.

After all this time, he's the one beside me.

His drops out of the cyclone of names flying around my head, and I try to laugh, but my rag just hangs there unwrung and heavy, like it holds a full bucket of old grey dishwater. I try moving my right arm but nothing happens. I try to move my left arm and it won't do much better, like I'm tethered to the bed. The room is right dark and there's whirring and beeping going on all the time. It gets on my nerves, so I let go of myself. Then the popcorn pops and spits and zings the corn clouds around again like they're shot from some corn gun, a corn cannon, maybe.

"Something's not quite right," I hear him say to somebody. "Something's wrong."

Hank's eyes are so blue. I remember thinking that in the dark. I remember thinking his eyes are the color of ocean water, and he's a sailor bound for the blue Pacific—a place I never expect to see. I just wanted someone I chose. I didn't think it mattered how long I'd have him. Just long enough. Those blue eyes. It's no wonder he ended up on the ocean. In the ocean. Blue eyes. Blue. Blue. Blue.

The blue of his eyes makes me drop out of my body into a waterless float that tries to suck me down. This must be what it felt like to drown. This is what he felt.

Then somebody plugs me in like that lamp Fanny had in the waiting room, the one that was a white horse reared up under the shade and trimmed in gold filigree lines, and the shock rides through me just like a big white horse, its hooves stomping me from inside my chest, trying to climb out of me like I'm the deep mud hole it got stuck in. And then it tries again, its big head swinging, its chest rising, its mane slinging like feathers as light as his hooves are heavy. Then it's finished. The big white horse climbs out of my chest and up through the ceiling of my room, and I hear the beeping again. The whir and the beep and the click, click, click, and it seems like a family of squirrels skitters and slides away across the floor pushing some big box on wheels and mumbling words about "blue," something about a blue coast. Or a blue coat maybe. I slip off, close to the edge, the little noises only a mind's touch away. ■

THE LONG WEEPING

JESSIE VAN EERDEN

I stand at the hand pump in the grove, young, maybe ten, having run from the signs of dying. Under the small shingled roof on the cement slab, the iron pump is smudged by creatures that licked it in the night, coons and cats and the rumored black bear. My jelly shoes are too tight over ankle socks and the downy hair on my legs prickles up, for the spring chill lingers in that threshold of time when the daffodils darken and the lilacs begin to make everything sweet and wet. Church has now let out and tall tired people spill into the churchyard, but I slipped out in the middle of the closing prayer, with Matthew who now pumps the handle, banging it against its base, coaxing the deep water to spout in the basin and arc higher and higher to my lips. I know he and I probably love each other, like two animals that trust one another's dusty smell. His body is simply like mine in height, in muscle, though his face is more like a baby's and so he is mean to seem older, but he wears meanness as if he has wrapped in a gauzy curtain, spun around and around, and made off with it: a boy pumping water in his see-through costume of meanness for a girl afraid of the signs of dying. One sign is the divot in the pillow on the camphor-smell bed that the women murmur about—somebody's mother with a long grey braid left a skull's impression like the bear-impress in the leaf pile, in the grove where it is said to sleep. Another sign is the man going blind singing only what he remembers of hymns, another is hipbone grinding hipbone with no cartilage to quiet the sound, another is each leg caked in pantyhose that plasters over the blue-veined skin that still breaks out at the sleeve, on the hands, and then there's the balding heads or the limp hair trying to remember its home perm and the dead jobs that do not pay enough because there are signs someone is taking money from the till at the Wash n Shop to get skirt sets for her girls, the girls just a little smaller than I, holding hands going to the church outhouse with lattice around it and airfresheners and tiny spiders weaving homes in the surplus toilet paper tube hollows. Maybe these girls are running too, I know my sister has run—by now she has made it to the car, finally free to scratch her itchy pits she has begun shaving, in a sleeveless dress not fit for the chill and so she jams her arms into the snap-up jean jacket, a hand-me-down from one of the girls bigger than I. My sister has stolen the keys from our mother's purse, she turns the ignition to hear Casey Kasem's countdown, to let the radio pull her into the world, toward names like Madonna and Prince and away from the old names: Harold, Don, Eliza, Gaye, Debbie, Sue, Walter, Jean. The seat's vinyl must be cool on her legs, the steering wheel sure in her grip, and something is saying to her *Don't waste any time getting here,* to where the living are, in the world of the radio and *Seventeen Magazine* where no one is old or wears polyester dresses, where your life will finally begin.

I turn to the spouting stream that Matthew has conjured with strength that equals my own. He is still pumping the handle, his baby face ruddy, his thoughts wholly unknown to me despite the commingling of our animal musk. Briefly, both of us watch the miracle at the spout that comes from the deep aquifer where snow has drenched down and seeped past dormant trillium roots, down past worm and centipede burrows, into networks of sandstone and clay, slate and sediment, to a breathspace that opens for water to pool in secret. For the rest of my life I will remember the taste of the water that somehow says *Don't waste time on water that is not water, on thirst that is not thirst.* The churchyard people are heavy with imminent egg noodles and beef, a nap, a still and lacquered afternoon when flies buzz, naps like dying-practice (for the rest of my life I will fear the death-kernel in naps and will wear myself out like a flapping terrified bird just to push through afternoons). I bend to the stream of water that meets my lips like a long weeping kiss, and right then, with my face in the small echo chamber of the basin, I hear my name, *Jess,* called from the water. I'm startled and I shoot up and look around. I hear it again, this time from the gravel lot across the road. It's my sister standing beside the car, sullen in the lilac-wet, in the jean jacket, draining the battery to listen to the radio. She hollers for me again, she must want to leave or must want me to hear the top hit. All at once I long for her and long for the water too and cannot help but bend to the iron basin again with its apparition of cobwebs now made visible by the water and sagging, the basin with tiny bug bodies and leaves, and still it seems that my name has come from the water spout, as if the water itself has named me and known me already, and I am small and not my own, not some new creature who has lit out and escaped, not so unlike the ones dying. Soon Matthew will push me aside for his turn, his shove the only way we ever know how to touch, but I am bending and drinking again, the water so cold, and I drink the name given to me, so cold I am startled again. Soon Matthew will push me away, soon I will barrel down the little hill to the tinny car radio to crowd in the driver's seat beside my sister's body and hear the top hit, but I feel like weeping. And I drink and I drink. ■

WHERE YOU ARE PLANTED

AMANDA JO RUNYON

Today is Tuesday. At 11:45 on Tuesday mornings, the residents of the Richland Hill Psychiatric Rehabilitation Center gather at the dining hall. We stand in bunches on the linoleum, shuffle our house shoes inside faux marble squares. The ones in front push their faces into the door and spread grins against the glass. Tiny puddles form at the corners of lips and surprised eyes scan the room for Sheila. We don't wait long before Sheila appears from the kitchen. She rubs one hand on her apron and uses the other to shove contrary strands of silver hair into a net before she turns the latch to let us in. We squeeze into a crooked line.

On Tuesdays we are introduced to the soup of the week. It will be lunch and dinner today, and whatever is left will be kept for days in a metal keg among untidy stacks of Styrofoam bowls and plastic spoons on the hall table. Today we have ham and bean stew. Sheila welcomes each guest by announcing the dish as they pass, bowls at their chest.

"Damn it," Charlie mutters from behind me when there are only two people between Sheila and us. Charlie is my roommate. She is exactly half my age. She is short for seventeen, and she bounces on the balls of her feet as she talks.

"Damn it," Charlie says again, bouncing closer to my ear. Tuesday is Charlie's favorite day. She always hopes for potato soup. She told me once that her mother made a loaded potato soup chocked full of cheese and bacon, and it was so good each bite felt like a little bit of sin. Sometimes, she said, they'd have a pot so big the whole family could eat on it for a week. It's what Charlie was having for dinner the day her mother died. She told me she couldn't leave the kitchen, not even after her father told her about the crash, until she'd scraped the last bit of creamy potato from the pot. Afterward her stomach ached and she threw up bacon bits during the funeral. So far, Sheila has not made potato soup.

The first time I came to Richland Hill, I had a room to myself. It was small and neat, and so empty it made me nervous. I filled the space with a collection of clipped blooms and pebbles from the garden and kept them in vases made of cafeteria milk cartons.

This time I asked my case worker for a roommate. Darlene is probably fifty with frosted hair that curls on her shoulders. She doesn't wear scrubs like the other staff. She wears jeans and pastel sweatshirts and Keds that squeak when she walks. When I asked for a roommate, she said the clients with double rooms already had roommates. Darlene calls us clients instead of patients. She said I needed the peace, anyway, that I needed time to think and to rest. She said this time I should fill the room with memories of my family, think back to who I was before I was sick.

On day one of my individual sessions, I told Darlene that I had spent the night trying to remember. I couldn't sleep. My room was quiet and sterile and kept me up all night with its dustless corners and Pine Sol floors. When I did drift off, I dreamed a whisper, dry and harsh, scratching around my head. I dreamed of piles of laundry that called my name. I dreamed of hanging from the fabric strands of a giant mop. On day two, I told Darlene I needed something to look at, to put my hands in, so my afternoon plans included gathering buckets of dirt. I would plant pansies near the window. Darlene said I could move in with Charlie. She said she didn't think she could find two people more opposite in the whole state of Kentucky, but in Charlie's room I sleep fine. She has a collection of paper clips she keeps in a two-liter Mountain Dew bottle on the dresser. She talks all night, even in her sleep.

After lunch on Tuesdays we have Group Talk in the Garden Room. The Garden Room is really a concrete patio with three glass walls. There is no air conditioning, only the gentle whir of two box fans opposite the circle of chairs. I settle into a folding chair close to the glass, and I wonder where they have Group Talk in the winter. It is June. They will send me home again before I have the chance to find out.

This Tuesday it is raining outside of the Garden Room. Blowing sheets of water slosh on the glass and weigh down the heads of geraniums on the other side. The fans blow the smell of the summer storm into our circle. It is fresh and warm and settles on our clothes and skin in a fine mist.

Lady Jane is our speaker this Tuesday. Lady Jane has pale yellow hair she keeps cut close to her ears. She has pictures of blue and red birds painted on her arms like sleeves. She has been at the center the longest and leads Group Talk once a month. She begins a prayer in a voice that sounds too hard to belong to someone so colorful. I rest my head against the glass wall of the Garden Room. There is a pink hydrangea bush, its flowers plump and dripping, leaning against the glass next to me. I push my cheek against the wall and imagine I can feel its petals, smooth and damp against my skin.

■ ■ ■

My Gran grew beautiful hydrangeas. They surrounded her porch, pink and blue bushes tall enough to spill onto the wooden planks. In a rainstorm like this one, she would sit out on the swing, sipping coffee and making pencil scratches in the puzzle book she kept in her apron pocket. I would curl up beside her and study the blossoms, confused by how the biggest ones were a pale mix of colors.

"How do they decide whether to be pink or blue?" I asked her once when I was a child, my legs beneath me on the swing and my head on her shoulder.

"It's not up to them," she told me. "It's up to the soil."

"That's not fair," I said.

Gran chuckled, laid her pencil in her lap, and pulled me close. "That's just nature, honey. You've got to bloom where you are planted."

■ ■ ■

When I got married, my husband bought us a home on Black Stone Court, where all the houses looked the same. I spent my honeymoon trying to recreate my Gran's garden in our new yard. My husband carried bags of soil over his shoulder, handed me the trowel, helped me up when I'd kneeled so long on the ground my legs were numb. He fussed with the dirt I tracked in the house. He never liked a mess. I filled the earth with seeds and bulbs. I put marigolds and zinnias in the front yard, black-eyed Susans and peonies in the back. I planted one hydrangea bush outside my bedroom window. It bloomed blue for one year, and then it died.

■ ■ ■

Visitation follows Group on Tuesdays. We are free for the evening to wait in our rooms for family members to bring backpacks full of cookies and cheap shampoo and paperbacks. The ones without visitors gather in the Rec Room to play Rook or watch television shows where people bid on bins of garbage hoping to find something valuable.

The first time I was here, my husband came every Tuesday. He brought folded sheets of construction paper with sloppy crayon hearts and love from the kids. He brought stories of botched dinners and ruined laundry. He ran down the daily schedules I knew by heart. Breakfast, school, band practice. He asked if I was sleeping. I would be fine, he was sure, if I could just get some rest. I didn't belong here, he said. The kids needed me. I should think of them, think of home, and get better.

This time he doesn't come every Tuesday. When he does visit, he sits on my bed, grinding his thumbs into the palms of his hands. He kicks at the dirty socks on the floor.

Last month, for my thirty-fourth birthday, my husband planned a barbeque. We ate steaks and potatoes stacked with onions and green peppers. Our neighbors were there. Their children chased our children around the pool and fell laughing on the grass. It was just what I needed, my husband said, a night of fun and relaxation. I sat in a lawn chair where my garden used to be. He brought me cake and wine. I dropped red velvet crumbs into my lap and they made red streaks across my legs. I didn't clean it up.

When everyone left, my husband put the kids to bed and he settled in front of the television. I climbed into our bed alone and cut my wrists with the blade from his bathroom razor. I drifted into sleep as blood seeped into our mattress. *What a mess I've made,* I thought.

■ ■ ■

My husband doesn't come this Tuesday. I wilt on the bed. Charlie is back from the Rec Room and she is bouncing by the dresser. *Next week,* she is saying. *Next Tuesday we will have potato soup.* ■

LET EVENING COME

KAREN SALYER MCELMURRAY

I have a garden that is a tangle, not of sweet peas, but of sunflowers and black-eyed Susans and echinacea spilling over a bank on the patio. As I sat out there last evening sipping my wine and watching the sky, I was jubilant. Marriage equality at last, after legal battles spanning forty some years. Love is love is love. But not two weeks ago, in a church in Charleston, a young man's act of rage took the lives of nine people. Another church in Richmond, Virginia, and some man banging the walls with a metal pipe while he shouted racisms at the congregation. And Thursday morning, a black church burned down in Charlotte, North Carolina.

I remembered a line from Voltaire about garden-minding and some days I want that to be enough. How can I use my voice in a way that matters without adding to the chaos of the world? I want to believe that beauty and a voice on a page and prayers even are enough. I want the power of quiet voices.

Some of my earliest memories are of voices. Sunday mornings. A church house, but I'm not sure where in eastern Kentucky I was. I was little enough to have the world be a floor and feet and things they gave me to keep me busy. Paper fans with Jesus and hymn books to stack into forts and towers. I also remember windows open to summer air. A bulletin board with how many attended, so I was old enough for numbers. And the sound of voices rising. It was the kind of church where people went up front and knelt and prayed all at once, a song-prayer, a collision of whispers. Quiet voices. *Heal her, Lord. Listen. Praise.* And later, in my memory, people waved arms toward heaven or ran around the room or fell out, their bodies shaking. It was a church to scare a child into belief or its absence.

Over the years, I've gone to a dozen kinds of churches trying, maybe, to understand what those prayer-voices were really saying. Quaker meetings. Mass. A temple blessing with yak butter and prayer flags. I've lit candles for the Blessed Mother in cities all over. Gone to a nunnery on the outskirts of a village in Greece where I lit candles to the Virgin of the Three Martyrs. Climbed to the grand, echoing Sacre Coeur at Montmartre. Gone to a roadside church of the Pentecost as I drove miles of backroads toward Harlan County, when I went back to visit the grade school I went to when I was a kid. All of it a faith from childhood left behind long ago.

My faith has been replaced by a variety of other voices. The word soul, someone said to me a couple years back, is a cliché. Better to think of faith as a secular experience, someone else said. Or this: spiritual writing won't sell. And this: all that talk about belief, it sounds so flakey. The charismatic churches of my early childhood represent to many a mishmash of uneducated with a dash of pagan thrown in there for good measure. *I'm surprised,* a student said to me on the phone the other day, *that you've kept your accent from where you come from. Why,* I asked. *Oh, people don't respond to me very well when I say I come from the mountains.* I've kept my voice, my heart, my faith, but I've kept it all in my pocket, a breviary of which I am dubious and curiously ashamed.

What would it look like if I took my faith out of its hiding place and held it in the palm of my hand? An origami bird. A polished red stone in the shape of a heart. The book I'm working on, dozens of little fragments about fire. The first fire I remember. A little girl they told about when I was little, how she fell face forward into the fireplace and her daddy grabbed hold and pulled her out, neither one of them a bit hurt by the flames. They told how it was a miracle.

Thomas Merton said, "we are living in a world that is absolutely transparent and the divine is shining through it all the time." I long for this to be true, but all I can think about this last week are the faces of those nine souls, shot by a twenty-two-year-old white supremacist boy who could very well have lived down the road from the church house I went to when I was little. I want to sign up for programs to teach me how to be a social worker. I want to go to divinity school and take up preaching. I want to dig holes and plant trees. I want to walk dogs in the park and speak to no one at all.

Or, as my friend Sonja Livingston writes, "The not knowing where it all will lead, the faith required to make art, the vastness of possibility, and all that we have no control over...the part that exists without flash or banter, the quiet part, the part we most need."

I come back to it, again and again. The open book. The blank page. I look for it, the thing beneath the thing. The moment underneath the chaos and despair. The ghost in the bones. A poem read aloud like a prayer. ■

TINTAGEL

Roaming through Cornwall, we saw
the sign of Tintagel and followed
a narrow road to the cliff-hung village.
The castle ruin, a long walk down, was
fornent the treacherous promontory
above the relentless, pulsing sea.
But, only crumbling walls stood fast
with sea winds blowing through.
I visioned Arthur, knights, round table,
and golden Guinevere by his side.
But Arthur is not here, I thought,
nor romance nor token of chivalry.
Then, in my mirror, driving back
a man floated, helmeted and visored,
sending a jolt through my doubting heart,
as he spurred his Honda 'round us, and
he, and we, and Arthur were all gone.

LOYAL JONES

WITHIN THE MUDSLIDE

We found a creation,
a totem pole carving
of salmon under earth.

The cedar spawns its eyes,
circles enchanting us
to recall an elder.

He must have swum oceans
like quick sockeye feeding
on lice and dragonflies.

And he built it, this lodge
emerging through the slide,
to smoke fish on alders.

And it is enormous,
as if he drained the sea
to fortify its planks.

So we reconstruct it
and all of his totem,
resurrecting his tale.

ANDREW JARVIS

SPEAKING OF LINEAGE

JACKSON CONNOR

Don't mention the rest of us punched silent
rivets in his cell walls, us proteins that rebar his
brickface, that buttress his architecture now warm,
now capable, now built of the junkyard dead.
—Jaswinder Bolina

It's hard to wake in the morning to poverty and despair and not want to blame our fathers. Look at mine, for instance, handsome enough, fit, smart as all hell, his own hands the size of God most of my life, and just happy to be here. Him, wrapped up in country music, and just fine with the way things are. *If the sun don't come up tomorrow,* Mom made him a t-shirt when I was eight, *people I have had a good time*, a Hank Williams Jr. song. Other phrases come to mind, lines that define his character, tell me how tough he is, how tough his mother was, how no matter how bad times got, she could always find a way to smile through things. All of this, too, is at the heart of my approach to the world, never necessarily concerning myself with home equity or a retirement plan, never fully understanding the difference between escrow and a bridge loan, never thinking beyond the day's concerns as long as there was something to laugh about come evening. The t-shirt has long since become a household rag, then a shop rag, and then lining for the trash can, and I doubt my folks have thought of it for some time, but if my family had a crest, if my dad had a tombstone, if our collective unconscious had a tattoo, no doubt, they would all be etched thick with those Hank Jr. lyrics.

He and his two sisters used to carry chunks of cast iron to bed with them, heated in the wood stove, actual irons Grandma Ruby used to smooth strangers' laundry. A non-electric iron—something entirely foreign to me—in a house without electricity, even into the 1950s. He never complained about this, but speaks of it with that restfully tilted head and scrunched cheek one has during a nostalgic fit, not quite smiling, not quite longing, not quite in this moment. Nostalgia is the damnedest part about being human, always telling us who we are, often keeping us from what we want to be. Grandma Ruby pulled the irons from the woodstove, snugged them up in towels, tucked the towels to her kids' chests, and layered them with blankets. This on the coldest, most tightly snowed-in days.

If Dad and his sisters had had a television at moments like that, they could have tapped into *Leave It to Beaver*. They could have watched *Father Knows Best*. Instead, they had the smoky glow of oil lamps, a fifty-yard trudge through the muddy yard to the outhouse, a crossword puzzle book, sometimes a jigsaw puzzle. Suburbia was supposed to be everywhere. The very word *America* meant a *cul de sac* and a station wagon to much of the country, but, truth be told, Dad never thought of himself as poor either.

The poor kids at his school sometimes had shoes, sometimes had no shoes. They lived in lean-tos or an abandoned bus, one family in a cave—a mother, three kids, the products of broken promises, some kind of mental illness, and hard luck; the mother had no idea where to seek help or even what to ask for if she had. But Dad could always find something to smile about, despite this backdrop of actual poverty, of barely human, entirely un-American lives. He played baseball, of course, made the wrestling team, had this kind of attitude—*I'll do this homework if it don't waste my time*—all the way through high school, and some teachers respected that, while others wanted the world to be my way or the highway, and they, after all, held the gradebook and were not interested in blind justice nearly as much as dumb obedience and mute conformity. He's a smart dude, no doubt about that, but he had no practical need for anything other than the ancient worn-out second-base mitt or a fishing pole and maybe a campfire to sit around, telling stories. He had, that is, learned to separate the world from the rot, which is all Socrates asked of his own students.

Toughness, of course, is at the heart of it all, this life. Dad's older sister Jan, hard as limestone, serious as a river maple, played softball. Western PA fast pitch, women who are fully equipped smokers and chewers and drunks, full of dirty language and bad ideas. Jan wore a thin catcher's mitt, so she could have a better feel for the ball. Dad, home on leave from the Navy, spent his weekend watching Jan catch a three-day tournament. The first game, she caught Jenny McGraw, who pitched like hell was chasing that ball and she was helping it get away. One foul tip shot back and jammed the tip of Jan's finger through the leather, tore it wide open, exposing a splintered bone, twisted ligaments, blood, meat. Jan walked across the street to the hospital, a napkin from Ruby's picnic basket holding the mess together. The doctor had set her bones before, and he sure wished he had some place to sneak off to, but probably realized she'd find him all the same.

He stitched her up, splinted her finger, and said, "Now, you might never play softball again. Certainly, you'll never catch. Come back in a few weeks and we'll have a better idea about long-term care." Jan set her jaw, rolled her eyes, thanked him, settled the bill, walked back across the street and finished the tournament. She caught Jenny McGraw and a couple others just like her all weekend, never once mentioning the pain, never once glancing at her finger. And if you'd a asked her about it, she'd a dropped her head and furrowed her brow, I'm certain, set her jaw, and said, "What's it to you?"

Jan set her jaw, rolled her eyes, thanked him, settled the bill, walked back across the street and finished the tournament.

The broken finger is a story of Jan's toughness, true, but it's also a story of Dad's own toughness. Of his modesty, too, how he claims he could never be as tough as his big sister, but look at his scars, listen to how he doesn't complain, ever, and you know he's tough. You know this story is about him. It's all of our story back Home. When I tell this story to friends, to coworkers, to acquaintances, I want them to know without my having to tell them that someday, I too, hope to catch a softball tournament with a freshly broken bone bouncing around inside my glove.

■ ■ ■

My mom, my sister, and I ride along with Dad to Ohio on a work trip. We stay in a motel room while he's in the field on mobile drill rigs. He's an electrical engineer for Chicago Pneumatic Tool, which means most days he wears a short-sleeved shirt with buttons and a breast pocket, but once in a while, he goes to Ohio or Texas and wears overalls. The drive from Venango County, Pennsylvania, to the other side of Ohio takes four hours, but people back Home are not travelers, vacationers, roamers, so this part of Ohio is the other side of the world, a galaxy far far away. Like this: channel three is on channel eight, channel twelve doesn't exist, and outside the window: no hills anywhere. The whole world is a horizon, endless possibility in every direction. Terrifying.

One afternoon, the sky turns green and a bright white squall line roils in from somewhere we've only seen on maps. New weather patterns to us, and this one, the radio says, could lead to a tornado.

A tornado! That's the neatest thing my sister and I have ever heard. Mom, on the other hand, does not jump from bed to bed high-fiving with us. We watch some big old hail in a dark midday. Some rain washes a couple weeks' worth of dust off the outside world. The wind picks up. The wind dies down. Rain falls.

We tire of waiting for a tornado and turn instead to the motel television with its channels on the wrong channels. The sky outside grows lighter and eventually darker again with late afternoon. Dad comes home earlier than we expect with a gash on his forehead above his right eye. New excitement after a bust tornado warning. He's been hit in the head with a ball-peen hammer—I plan my vengeance. He's been hit in the head with a hammer by accident—I postpone my vengeance. Chicago Pneumatic Tool, his home company, had asked him to go to the hospital to get stitches. He and the hammer-swinger went to the bar instead to get gin and tonics. At the motel, he's bright-eyed, and when we ask for a detailed description of what happened to his head, he says, "Well, I was sorting bobcats and I got a hold of a mountain lion." His standard response to any visible wound, and I swear, when I think of that cut I hear Hank Williams Jr. *if the sun don't come up tomorrow*, even if I don't mean to hear it, *people I have had a good time.*

He puts a Disney Band-Aid over a gaping wound, and we say, "But doesn't it hurt?"

He says, "Oh, it don't hurt."

Moments like this, we pick our heroes.

■ ■ ■

Modest, tough, handsome enough—you see? You see why we want to be our fathers? Then here's me, for instance, during the first year of a master's program that's thick with literary theorists, post-structuralism, post-modernism, post-everything tangible, a world full of the mind. Here's me, asked to write a paper about the effect of phenomenology on the Derridean concept of *différance*. Here's me responding with an essay about chewing tobacco in the steel mill. How clever I was: *chewing* tobacco, the product, *chewing* tobacco, the process. The noun, the verb, steel, *steel*, mill, *mill. Différance, difference, deference.* I mean, I got it, the theory. I simply refused to see the practical application of it. Rather, all I've ever wanted is to be worthy of a story my dad might tell to his dad Chuck or his Uncle Cecil should they meet again in the afterlife. So I ground the theory up with the steely dust, and the wood chips, the shit and the soil, the stories of desperate unprotected sex, sweaty Pennsylvania nights, grey I-80 running through our dark green hills. I had no actual motto, but if I had, it would have sounded like this: *I'll do this work if it don't waste my time.* I got B's in my theory courses, did fine in my lit courses, wrote and wrote and wrote for my writing workshops, and pounded my steel chest with the smooth river rock memories piled up by my father and his father before him, by his Uncle Cecil and all my own uncles sitting around the campfire, drinking a beer.

Dad's dad, a lifetime janitor, was an alcoholic, true, and somehow always already packed tightly into a glass ball turret, firing away at Jerry. Dad tells me his old man was *different* when he came back from the war. "This was before we had PTSD," he says, "so they called it shellshock, but he just never was the same." My dad shrugs after he says this. This is what I know of my grandfather—his best clothes were a new pair of overalls with a white, ovaled *Chuck* and a Pennzoil badge. He had to leave a wife and three young kids to fight in World War II. He drank Genesee beer and cheap whiskey, a straight-pipe Winston forever stashed between the crooked knuckles of his right hand. And the distant oily smell of a soapy mop bucket from the Rouseville refinery on the outskirts of Oil City, a plant where my dad would eventually work for a few years in polyester pants and a blue-striped yellow tie—where I would work for a long hot summer in long-sleeved green overalls and steel-toed boots. The refinery's gone now, the idea of it moved to Texas at the millennium.

My dad only ever met his grandfather, Chuck's dad, my great grandfather, once: face full of black, pocked gravel dug in a buckshot pattern around his face because he went to take a piss and fell off the train. Nor did Chuck know him well. I know nothing about my line before him, nor does my dad.

There is nothing to know, no one to ask. I have only one story of the oldest man: my dad, a child, standing on the dirt floor of the basement, wiggling the gravel around with his fingertips underneath the skin of that tired cheek. An upturned wooden egg crate. A bottle of whiskey. That's the origin of my species, my dad meeting his paternal grandfather once, for a hot minute one evening, a hobo, it's true, though we've never said that word between us, but handsome enough, kind, and funny, able to carry a tune—a falsetto though none of them necessarily called it that, rather they hummed and cracked jokes and continued the long process of smoking themselves to death. He had a wild imagination about what a heavy-set woman could do to a man in the dark that a skinny woman could never do by light of day. When they needed someone

I know nothing about my line before him, nor does my dad. There is nothing to know, no one to ask.

to sing higher, one of them would stand on that egg crate, balancing himself against the whiskey and warble out tunes from a distant unknowable land, even as the lyrics arose out of this Appalachian soil.

My great-grandfather abandoned Grandpa Chuck when he was three years old and sick, leaving him with the memory of a mother who had died giving birth to him, and a big sister who had been killed by a motor vehicle. The girl was my great-grandfather's prize for making it this far in life, his lifeblood connection to his wife, worth every effort to go on living. She was hit and killed by a Model T, if you can imagine that, along the washboard dirt road in front of their tiny house, and just as quickly everything was over, everything was gone. The oldest man was broken and none of us blames him. He left the world that had been built around him, for him, by him; he skidded and bounced along the crushed limestone gravel, passing on the story of the scars, God knows where or how he came to a rest. The point is: he was a tough old bastard, nonetheless. That's how he built Chuck, maybe, by walking away. That's how he built Dad. And here I am, for years with that sneer on my face, the stitches, the cauterized forearm, the chip off a bone floating around just beneath the surface on the back of my hand. And if you asked me, I'd tell you: *If the sun don't come up tomorrow, people I have had a good time.*

We've taught each other to endure, my folks and I, to smile at people who do us wrong such that they know that they can't get under our skin, even as they are always on our minds, always already winning. We tell each other little stories about outdoing the big guys, about being not as well off, sure, but somehow happier than the lawyers, somehow more cunning than the bankers, somehow more worldly wise than the doctor, stitching up, once more, our forearms, our fingers, our faces. Believing, always with our eyes lolling around like a calf tethered by lack and desire in these hills, that *money can't buy us happiness*. And, though, technically, that's true, there's always a sad, misconstrued truth to any cliché. *Money can't buy us happiness*, but money does buy us choice. And choice often means the ability to improve our diet, keep our skin clear, allow us to take a weekend off when we come down with strep throat, afford us leisure time with our children or violin lessons, or the opportunity to teach them something other than how to endure, how to be tough, how to sit there and take it, whatever it is that comes at us.

■ ■ ■

"Uncle Cecil," Dad tells me, "Had hands the size of God." He says, "Him and Mary used to have great big rabbit pens down there at the farm—I don't know if you remember seeing them when you were little—and when I was a kid, Cecil would take me down there and let me pick out dinner. I'd pick up a rabbit like a dish I didn't want to break, and I'd hand it to Cecil, and he'd grab it by the neck and *phhhllehhp* pull its head off and toss it out in the weeds."

Sometimes in conversations about role models or good health, this story comes up, sometimes we're talking about family or the supermarket, about bird dogs or the body's precarious balance. I envy Dad, who had the chance to learn from this man on the farm, his oldest role model, who held sixteen penny nails between his teeth by the dozens. I imagine a simpler time, without debt or desperation, without kids or commitments, without a high efficiency water heater, true, but also without the fear and confusion that accompanies replacing a high efficiency water heater. I imagine a past as if the stress of financial woe were an invention of the twenty-first century, something created directly to haunt me and those I care so deeply about, rather than the recycled business of every successive generation. I imagine myself, too, someday having the strength, the wherewithal, and the necessity to rip an animal's head right off its neck.

Dad and I stood in the bottom yard of my folks' camp along the Allegheny River, each holding a dead rabbit we'd shot for dinner. He'd just told me about Cecil again, the thirtieth, fortieth time, a story I never tire of, a story which always opens another room in that house of Dad's unknowable youth, always some new detail. This time it was about Cecil's shoulders. "Wide as a man door and taller than any ladder I'd ever climbed," he told me.

I said, "Well, here we are."

He said, "Give it a try?"

"But how?"

He shrugged, "Twist it till it ain't attached."

I felt as though I were being duped, and worried that such a feat was impossible, that he could laugh at me now and forever, *remember the time you tried to tear off the rabbit's head? Thought you'd sprain your wrist turning the thing*. But, like I say, my dad would never dupe anyone into anything – he's legit, sincere, nothing to lie about. Then the head was in my hand, popped right off more easily than most jelly jars. I asked Dad if I could do his too. We traded rabbits. He tossed the first head into the tall grass and held the limp body by its hind feet. I threw the second head into the tall grass like I'd seen my father do and we walked up to the camp, him talking about rabbit meals he'd had, me thinking about Cecil, wondering how the world might revere or, at least, acknowledge me, or just take note of these bone crushing hands at moments like this.

■ ■ ■

My hands today are cracked and dry and cold after hours running a miter saw at seven below zero with wind chill. I don't know if I'd call them cuts, but I can see through broken skin in two-dozen tiny spots. I deal with them like this: if I must look at them, I look away mad. If you catch me looking at them, I scowl at you noncommittally, angry at something you don't need to understand. This particular look builds on whatever look I might have been wearing already this morning: concern that I can't pay my bills, resentment I feel towards a college student with a sixty dollar haircut, a shrugged off PhD in a field flooded with PhDs. My hands hurt, but nobody needs to know about it—that's what I know about injury and illness: it's between me and my god.

My hands now are damaged and sore, because I work on a construction crew to supplement the increasingly pitiable pay of the adjunct instructor. My dearest friend, who happened to earn his PhD with me, had graduated high school with soon-to-be doctors and lawyers, had worked on the yearbook staff with a future renowned Hollywood writer and director. After earning his PhD in English, he considered a career as a lawyer. My friends from Home are in steel mills, on road crews, working for contractors. I went to Cub Scouts with a guy who shot a cop a year after graduating high school, who died in prison this year. None of my buddies' parents worked in any capacity for a law firm. My buddies' and my names have been the occasional subject of arrest columns, but always the litigant, never the practitioner.

My poet friend, my successful friend, my dearest friend, whom my children call Uncle Wind-er, whose poetry is the song of my life, cooks us dinner when he visits. He helped me build the per-gola out back, plant the garden out front, hang some drywall in the basement. He's quite handy for a poet. Some days we sit by the fire drinking whiskey and cheap beer until dawn. If I have one leg up on him, it's that I have spent a lot more time in construction than he, such that I run a circular saw more quickly. Our lifework—his and mine—is writing. We're writers through and through. No doubt. His second book of poetry has been out for over a year, and I've had a handful of essays and short stories published since we met. Nonetheless, when I hand him the nippers—squarish headed pliers used to remove nails—he moves slowly from nail to nail, sometimes using both hands, while I rip them out with either hand at awkward angles.

What I want for my life is to carry around my own books of poetry and prose, to read fa-mously at famous readings in front of famous people. What he has. And, yet, I strut around, foolishly, taking sad, simple pride in the skittering rhythm of worn out finish nails on concrete. This is my legacy, these big, strong hands.

My dear poet friend flew out of our frozen Appalachian town early January and, that evening, sat on his apartment balcony at his R-1 institution city. His second book of poetry and dozenth essay, both recently receiving national acclaim. His life—and I mean this literally and in all other ways—in his own hands. He abides by annual physicals and occasional questions for his cousin the doctor, with visits to his physician for any more immediate concerns. He was raised practically: be smart, plan ahead, approach with care. Far from a hypochondriac, he takes preventative medicine when he feels a sniffle, sleeps in late if he's got an ache. He's going to live forever, I hope, and rightfully so, though his own father is aging over the phone, just as mine is aging over the phone. Though his father's father died when he was ten, just as Chuck died when I was ten. He's going to grow old with care and prudence while I scowl at the nurse and tell him to mind his own business.

■ ■ ■

Meanwhile, there's Grandpa Chuck, not so old in retrospect, gripping at his left arm and scowling at the pain, sitting on the couch, trying to wheeze or whatever he could manage. Grandma Ruby stomping out the cigarette that had fallen from his mouth and saying, "Chuck, please."

Chuck saying, "Goddamnit, Ruby. Put down the phone." And Chuck thinking, *finally,* his life flashing slowly before him, a haze of blue and grey smoke against the tar-yellowed drop ceiling, the greying gun cabinet in the bed room, the three grown kids, "two daughters and a slug," as he would say. *Finally, I can rest. I can put my mind to rest.*

"I don't need no goddamned doctor," Chuck tells Ruby, and that long dusty road pulls a wobbly black Model T over his big sister again and again in his sickness and health, in his youth and his age, and that oldest man pours himself into a bottle and hands Chuck to Cecil, crawls into a boxcar and tries not to roll when he hits the ground, and all those rabbits and all those heads tossed into the tall grass with the bills we can't pay, the future we can't provide, the myth of retirement, the happiness we would try to buy, even if we knew the sun wouldn't come up tomorrow. *Finally,* he thought, the fading blue overalls and the scuffed black shoes holding him in this resting place. Him rolling into a ball to fill that glass cage in the belly of the bomber, the thin air frosting the world around him as he, in turn, lit the world on fire. The Earth always unsteadily rising up underneath him, promising to catch him restfully should he fall from this cradle. *Finally,* his last fucking smirk, I'll just goddamned bet you when the EMTs clamored out of the siren, out of the blazing cab of the van, out of the spinning lights and camphor, strapping him to the gurney, and *if the sun don't come up tomorrow,* no more soapy mop bucket and oil everywhere. The black pocked gravel moving now beneath his own fingertips, sliding around his own cheekbones, his teeth, the dirt-floor memory of Home. *Finally,* a last sad lyric blinked out above the wooden egg crate, an homage to everything about himself he'd never know, nor know who to ask about, *all of your damn horses and all of your damn men,* he must have thought, not quite tough enough to cry at this moment, or maybe the pain was enough to bury what's worse, the dust and the grit and the gravel and despair. ■

HIGH SCHOOL CAFETERIA IN EASTERN KENTUCKY

Into the crowd of siblings, cousins
once and twice removed,

ballplayers and their girls,
third-generation teachers,

walked Johnny Montgomery,
dark skin at least as strange

as his last name in these parts.
He opened up

a swath of silence that closed
incrementally

as he moved past. The quiet
was so great it buzzed the ear

and felt like a hand
clutching the throat.

He set down his tray
of square pizza and two cartons

of milk at the only open spot,
he on one end of the table, the oldest

Fultz boy on the other,
the one who'd stabbed his brother

in the local pool hall.
He looked up from his free lunch

and tilted his head to one side,
cuing the chatter to build again

as he took a large bite.
Johnny held chin down, eyes up,

the look of a child
eyeing a trinket.

Outside a murder of crows
flew and turned in unison.

C. LYNN SHAFFER

HATEFUL

my Granny said, her pleated
velvet cheeks aquiver
as we watched the battered
Fords and coal trucks

splatter gravel from the road
above the porch.
That's one thing
I can't abide.

I don't remember
who it was or what he did
that made my Granny spit
his name like chaw

into her jar, but I remember still
the boy who shot into my mind—
my mother called him hateful, too,
the way he'd hold himself

up high and hard there
in his daddy's store—
and how I wanted
what he had,

bone-weary as I was
of my own softness.

PAULETTA HANSEL

AN *APPALACHIAN HERITAGE* INTERVIEW

JESSIE VAN EERDEN

Jessie van Eerden's speaking voice is gentle, inviting, smooth as a creek stone. She's reading of prayers, of a woman wearing a black slip and smoking Pall Malls, of the "cloud of witnesses" from St. Paul's Epistle to the Hebrews, and her listeners are entranced, transported far from this dull classroom on the campus of East Tennessee State University. Van Eerden is here as part of the 2015

Appalachian Studies Association Conference, sharing a panel titled "Voice Lessons" with novelist and poet Darnell Arnoult, fiction and creative nonfiction writer Karen Salyer McElmurray, and fiction writer and editor Amanda Jo Runyon. The quartet is offering selections from their own work and discussing the concept of voice in creative writing and all the different types and pitches found in Appalachian literature.

Voice is, of course, an amorphous topic, hard to pin down, difficult to define. To quote former Supreme Court Justice Potter Stewart, "I know it when I see it," and I see it all over van Eerden's work. Her voice is lyrical, complex, ruminating—characteristics on full display in her sparkling debut novel *Glorybound* and in her many essays that have appeared in places like *Ruminate*, *Image*, and in *Best American Spiritual Writing*.

In a recent conversation, van Eerden and I discussed the sensual qualities her writing, of being haunted, and her role as director of West Virginia Wesleyan University's MFA in Writing Program.

■ ■ ■

JASON HOWARD: I've read your beautiful essay "The Long Weeping" [included in this issue of *Appalachian Heritage*] a few times now, and it's so evocative—I feel like it's almost a scene from my own childhood. Why did this moment in particular—the images, the people, the music—linger with you?

JESSIE VAN EERDEN: I am grateful to hear that this essay evokes something in you—that always feels like a real moment of contact when someone reads your work and sees himself in it. You and I may have had similar childhoods, but I am probably trying to evoke elements of childhood that might resonate with any reader, whether or not he or she grew up in a church with no indoor plumbing! I think moments of childhood sleep in us and they wake up when we read something that renders the consciousness of childhood faithfully. Children of the Eighties will likely remember the jelly shoes and Casey Kasem in the essay and find recognition there, and most will also find regular use of a hand pump very odd for that decade, but the recognition and strangeness are both on the surface—the particular moment lingers with me because I keenly remember it as a time when my life felt too big for me, as if it were swollen with all the lives of the older people in the Whetsell Settlement, my home community in rural West Virginia. I love the opening of Agee's *A Death in the Family*: "We are talking now of summer evenings in Knoxville, Tennessee, in the time that I lived there so successfully disguised to myself as a child." That notion feels true—children feel and remember so much more than we think, and they store stuff away in their old souls. When Agee describes the moment of his father watering the lawn and goes in so close to the sound and vision of the hose—the water "just a wide bell of film"—I feel my own childhood pulsing there, though my own dad would never have spent precious well water on the lawn. It's that moment of fullness, of realization that life is full to the brim and it is something you can lose. The sacredness and the grief well up together in such moments.

Jessie Van Eerden

JH: What else haunts you?

JVE: At the moment, I'm haunted by a recent reissue of Sally Mann's *Immediate Family*, a collection of photographs of her children in rural Virginia; the photos are stunning and blurry and dreamlike, with lots of inner life pulsating all over the place. I bought the book because of a thought-provoking essay of Mann's in the *New York Times* this past April in which she addresses the controversy over her work—I wasn't that familiar with her photos or aware that many people think she exploits her kids and reveals too much about them (they're often nude in the photos). Of all works of art, real connection happens for me most immediately with portrait photography, the kind of I-Thou contact that Martin Buber describes, instead of the I-It relationship that lets the photo remain an object. Faces and bodies in photos often feel very active and participatory in their being seen—they become a Thou to be met and reckoned with—and they can haunt you for days. Photos like hers that raise questions about ethical responsibility to your subject are particularly haunting because of how they resonate with writing work, with the responsibility we have to the people we write about, characters both invented and real. Mann's photos are all the more tender and uncomfortable because she's a mother photographing her children, so all the roles blur. This question of responsibility to our subjects opens to the larger question of the artist's responsibility to the world that we're here to bear witness to; the question itself probably haunts all artists. We are more global and connected than ever, of course—virtually—yet only by the thinnest of threads, it seems, which break if they're strained the tiniest bit. It's overwhelming, and I guess the way I often explore that overwhelming and baffling connection is by returning in my work to the small community I grew up in, to those musty houses where I went to youth group meetings and we had to go real slow up the gravel road in the dark because the black angus would crowd around the car and lick it and we couldn't see them, we had to be careful—those connections between people were the first and strongest I'd sensed so they still instruct me.

In a wonderful poem by West Virginia poet Irene McKinney, "Homage to Hazel Dickens," she writes: "Whether we go or stay, we've lost it./ The porch, the cold crocks of cream in the cellar,// the redbone hound in the yard, the wild azalea all orange/ and sweet, we've lost it standing here looking at it// this way." When you look at your home, the very stuff of your day, with a certain kind of gaze that recognizes the stuff is imbued with preciousness because it's fleeting, I think everything starts to haunt you—the faces of your freshmen composition students, your mailman who limps, the girls down the road who do each other's makeup on the front porch. Of course we can't look at things that way all the time, with that kind of gaze—we'd short circuit or explode and we wouldn't be able to tie our shoes for the ridiculous weeping! But the spiritual practice of writing is what trains us to see that way at sustained wonderful increments and to try to render what we see, to say *Look*. I think when you look at a piece of art that rises up in you and haunts you, it melds with the stuff already haunting around in your mind so that there's a real sense of interconnectedness, maybe wholeness.

JH: You're a very sensual writer—I keep thinking about how, in the essay, you describe "the divot in the pillow on the camphor-smell bed" and legs "caked in pantyhose." Where do you think your attention to the senses comes from?

JVE: It probably comes mostly from reading and being stunned again and again by writers who convey a sense of fatefulness, as the poet Li-Young Lee puts it, that sense of inevitability: *yes, that is exactly right, that image, that experience, my whole being thrums with how very right it is.* When I have that moment of having some sliver of experience of the world rendered so perfectly by a writer, all I think is 'I want to do that!' because it's such a magical experience.

I also got some good training in attending to the senses from growing up with a lot of hands-on garden work—a lot of touching of the world, digging potatoes, weeding carrots carefully so you didn't pull up the carrots themselves—and with three older creative siblings who were always making stuff like laser beams out Maxwell House coffee cans, pallet-and-tarp forts, kites, periscopes out of paper towel rolls. On the back of the kitchen cabinet door, my mom kept a list of things to do when we got bored so if we ever whined, she'd open the cupboard to her list and say, "Go make periscopes!" She always had the best ideas. (Today she called to tell me how to make my own deodorant, so she still has the best ideas!)

JH: Much of your writing—including "The Long Weeping" and your novel *Glorybound*—is heavily rooted in the spiritual, and you've had work featured in *Rock & Sling* and *Best American Spiritual Writing*. What has been your own experience with religion and the spirit, and how has it informed your art?

JVE: Talking about faith-informed writing feels similar to talking about place-informed writing: both kinds of writing are about the landscapes that forge your imagination. I don't think we have a lot of choice about what those landscapes are, or even about what our primary concerns are in our writing. It's hard to talk about personal experience with religion since it's just that, pretty personal, but I can say that for me it has to do with *unfoldment*—a word my friend and colleague Devon McNamara used the other day in regard to working through our tasks not as one works down a check list, robotically, but in a spirit of natural unfoldment. Isn't that beautiful? I apply it here to spirituality because it's something that keeps unfolding. Many of us who grew up fundamentalist in small churches, then went off to college and "got out in the world," whatever that means, often feel that the chapter on religion in our lives is closed and there simply to be written about and excavated as a thing of the past, the way you talk about your mom cooking with too much butter—endearing, but of course you use olive or coconut oil now, you have better sense. But it seems too easy to me to block off religion in that dismissive way. Religion is important to such a vast majority of people because it asks the hardest questions—we can flat out disagree over how it answers them if we want, and we can argue it's too packaged or narrow-minded, and also that the rigid answers can do a great deal of damage to people. But religion's questions about death, meaning, time, love—they are just as real as they are when they're posed by philosophy, art, physics. I grew up looking at those questions through the lens of altar calls and Bible studies and revivals, and it seems to me the lens continues to grow larger, still including those things but also other things.

Also, I grew up, in some ways, without such strict compartments (compartments the publishing market subscribes to, unfortunately: Spiritual Writing, Appalachian Writing, Paranormal Writing). Doing your hair and praying over somebody's tumor were activities that shared the same moment and the same room—talking to the beautician and talking to God, both seemed to be available and accessible auditors. Compartmentalism can cause trouble. For instance, a problem with faith-interested (as well as place-interested writing) is that it can be self-referential and tribal, or coded, and can close out those who are from other landscapes. Maybe the way you avoid that "clubbiness" is by focusing the heart of your work on the forging and firing action, on that lived experience of being shaped in your imagination, because that is shared by everyone, even if the active forces or landscapes vary drastically. But human formation and growth and development, when that is your subject you're getting down to a pretty deep root we all share.

JH: You wrote most of *Glorybound* when you lived in Seattle, far across the country from your native West Virginia, where the novel is set. Did you find that this physical—and perhaps emotional—distance informed your writing of the book?

JVE: Probably, yes. I remember that it was hard to hear the dialog, and it helped that I revised the novel during a few months when I was living back in West Virginia. Mainly though I wonder if time affects composition more than space does. In Seattle I had huge chunks of time to occupy that novel as I drafted it, because I had the great fortune of having a fellowship from *Image* that enabled me to write while teaching only one class at Seattle Pacific University. Now I live in West Virginia but I often have much smaller increments of time to really steep myself in the place of the novel I'm currently working on (this novel is also set in West Virginia) so I feel it's sometimes harder to conjure the West Virginia that is right outside my doorstep!

Also, I was in a writing workshop with Seattleites for a brief time while drafting *Glorybound*, and I remember they hated the first draft of the first chapter that opened with

Aimee Lemley in a low-cut blouse sitting on the cinder-block steps in front of her trailer. No way you can start a "southern" novel that way, they insisted—I didn't correct them that it wasn't a southern novel, it was a mountain novel, but, anyway, I was interested in their resistance. It was an interesting environment in which to try to depict a much-abused and much-stereotyped place where people do live in trailer parks (as they also do ten miles out of Seattle).

JH: In my own writing life, I think a lot about what Rainer Maria Rilke wrote in one of his letters: "A work of art is good if it has arisen out of necessity." Why was it necessary for you to write *Glorybound*?

JVE: That's one of the best questions to ask of any piece of writing. I ask it of my students constantly, and I ask it of myself always. If there is no urgency for me in a piece of writing, I move on (whether I'm reading it or writing it). Life is too short! Not that I don't read *fun* stuff—I'm not some kind of strict humorless reader (and maybe Rilke could've loosened up, who knows?)—but fun doesn't mean vacuous or self-indulgent. I remember in grad school it was fashionable to romp around with random stuff that interested you, word play, stunt essays, and much of it seemed self-indulgent to me, or hermetic, but maybe I just didn't understand it (even when I was the one trying to do it). Probably that's the case. I can say that I did feel a need to write *Glorybound*. It treats many of the themes I was obsessed with in essay-writing when pursuing my MFA in nonfiction, and the novel poured out more or less right after I finished my degree. For that novel, maybe on the surface I needed to write about patriarchy in the church or about the interior textures of people whom I feel are dismissed in our broader culture (Bible-reading girls cooped up in a trailer in West Virginia), but mostly I think I needed cede over the reins of a project to characters who could teach me how to make something whole, a unified world that could be a mirror for this real world. I needed to just learn more about that miraculous work—I'm still learning.

JH: You direct the West Virginia Wesleyan University Low-Residency MFA in Creative Writing program. What sets this program apart from other low-res programs?

JVE: Every program tries to be unique, and I think every program probably is unique! We have an embarrassment of riches in this country when it comes to opportunities to deepen one's writing in the company of other writers. We are lucky dogs. I naturally feel that Wesleyan's program is particularly unique, and maybe that kind of pride in what you're invested in is inevitable because you see it up close, you see it's the real deal. There are some stand-out qualities of the program for sure. First, it was founded by Irene McKinney, one of West Virginia's most important and most visionary poets, and she cast the tone for a rigorous and nurturing program, a balance that's not easy to achieve in an MFA program. Irene went back for her undergraduate degree when she was married with kids; in her words in her poem "At 24": "I was writing to save my life as I knew it/could be." That kind of vision of writing as salvific, as fulfillment of your deepest potential, as something you've waited to pursue and *need* to pursue, pervades the program, and I love that. The program also cultivates literature that's interested in place, though does not exclude writers for whom place is not a central concern of their work. We invite Appalachian writers like Ann Pancake, Maggie Anderson, Crystal Wilkinson, and Scott McClanahan to come and contribute to the ongoing conversation about what it means to make literature in this region for readers inside it and also beyond it. We stress good writing, period, but we do keep alive that strand of conversation about how to be vigilant against flat, stereotypical or sentimental writing about the region; how to convey the many kinds of Appalachias that exist and keep shifting; how to avoid getting too insular or tribal. We are intentional about inviting in minority voices of the region, Affrilachian voices in particular, to complicate a picture of a region associated mostly with whiteness.

Also, because I'm a practical person, I will note that the program is uniquely affordable among low-residency programs. It's important to us to keep it that way.

In the current economic and academic climate, it is common to discourage folks from enrolling in MFA programs. Maybe there's wisdom in that; who can really say? I feel such programs are like church services—almost *despite* all the infrastructure and ritual and trappings, real contact can happen, a vision at the altar can happen, incredible art can get made. I do feel the writers in our program receive superb feedback and keen attention to their work; I don't know that that's unique among MFA programs; I hope it's not. It may be unique that for the thesis manuscript we have four established writers who give pages and pages of feedback for each thesis, and three of us host a conversation about the manuscript with the writer—I feel that this emphasis on creating the best manuscript possible is a wonderful aspect of the program.

Honestly, no one needs an MFA program to write, but the context can be life-changing nonetheless.

JH: Who are some of your faculty members?

JVE: I am so fortunate to get to teach with a solid and generous group of core faculty and also with incredible circulating guest faculty. Some of the guest faculty have ties to Appalachia—Karen Salyer McElmurray, Carter Sickels, Mary Carroll-Hackett, Marie Manilla; some are fine writers from other places like Julia Kasdorf and Kim Dana Kupperman. Many low-residency programs have an on-site director but a far-flung faculty, but I am grateful to have these five core faculty members on campus with me so that we can collaborate to build each residency's curriculum and share ideas about mentoring students: Mark DeFoe, Devon McNamara, Richard Schmitt, Doug Van Gundy and Eric Waggoner. It feels like we are very much part of something together and not just "teaching in a program."

JH: Many of the program's students are either native or have ties to Appalachia. How do you think the program prepares them to contribute to the region's literary community and beyond?

JVE: As I mentioned, we do cultivate a vigilance here in favor of accurate and multidimensional depiction of the region, for students who do set their work in West Virginia and want to confront things like the devastation of mountaintop removal sites, the water poisoning of the fracking industry, the negligence of the chemical companies along the Elk River, or who want to explore the cultural and material poverty here explicitly, alongside the strong ties of family and significant regional themes like leaving and staying. But our requirements for our writing mentors is a record of fine writing and commitment to teaching, and we feel it's important to have an inflow of diverse writers from across the country, with many perspectives, so that the room doesn't get too stuffy or provincial. Irene McKinney's assessment in the first year of the program still feels true to me about many of the writers in the program: “Our students seem to feel very strongly that they are regional writers with a national audience.”

JH: As writers and writing teachers, we often talk a lot about voice. Do you approach your work with a particular voice in mind, or do you allow it to present itself as you write—in effect to surrender to what’s happening on the page?

JVE: Yes, I feel that voice as a topic is amorphous and complex, mystical even, but also quite practical in some ways. When you talk about use of multiple registers or the effect of Germanic and Latinate verbs, you get into very pragmatic, toolbox issues of voice. There is probably an inborn voice you’ve got going that you don’t have a lot of say about, though I don’t believe it’s wholly static—it gets to be born more than once. Isn’t it incredible really what goes into the making of a voice? It’s simultaneously collaborative and innate, in your DNA but also in the stuff you breathe in daily—the albums you love, the most recent book you puzzled over, the grandfather you worshipped and hated, the teachers who have helped speak you into being. But there is also the distinct voice in each piece of writing, and maybe we have to meet that voice with the other more comprehensive voice of our being so that each piece is really a synergism of sound. I don’t really know. The voice of the novel I’m working on now is quite different than that of my first and second, and it does seem like it’s a voice I had to find: it was somewhere just a little outside of the voice I already knew. I love your verb, *surrender*—it’s a much more active and rigorous posture than mere passivity. Surrender requires great love and attentiveness. ■

BAT HOUSE BLESSING

At dusk the bats emerge, two and two
and two from a hole in the eave invisible
until they appear, aureoles for the last light.

Their pivots and curtsies a jaunty dance,
we wonder if, like swans, bats mate for life.
We know our landlord would exterminate

and promise to keep this secret, yet we know
only rumors of rabid bats and vampire myth.
The Web separates bat lore from bat fact:

a single brown bat eats 600 mosquitos an hour;
females mother a single "pup," swinging
at its birth from her upside-down perch

to catch the babe in her tail and carries
him until he can see how to fend for himself;
whether colony, cloud, or camp, we fear them

less than they fear us. At dusk each day
we wait for them to fall silently two and two
and two from the eave to circle into the dark.

DONNA J. LONG

WHAT
WORK IS

DEAN MARSHALL TUCK

So up and down I sow them
For lads like me to find,
When I shall lie below them,
A dead man out of mind.
—A.E. Housman, A Shropshire Lad, *LXIII*

Randy's father rattled the classified section and held the paper an arm's length from his face, squinting as he prepared to read the ads aloud, a weekly ritual. Lying on the couch, Randy waited for him to begin. Instead, he lowered the paper. "Don't you reckon you ought to get to bed? Tomorrow's going to start early."

"I reckon."

"You reckon? I told Mr. Madison you'd be at his greenhouse at seven."

Randy stared at the ceiling fan.

His father began skimming the job postings. "Driver…no CDL needed. Machinist…on-site training." He paused. "You going to want breakfast?"

"Sure."

"You want me to wake you up then?"

"I got an alarm clock."

"Fine. Fine. It'll be ready after six. I'm going to bed." His father groaned as he rose from his chair, dropping the paper on the ottoman. "Suggest you do the same."

His father had spoken to Mr. Madison in church. Madison had mentioned how he could use good help transplanting tobacco, preferably not a Mexican.

Randy wouldn't mind the job too much, but it galled him to be coerced, guilted, or drafted into work. Farming was nothing new. He'd helped his dad farm since he was tall enough to top tobacco. He'd known hard work in his adolescent life—humid summers in tobacco fields and bulk barns. There was always work those summers, but since his father had given up farming a few years ago for a job at WOH Pharmaceuticals near Raleigh, Randy's duties had largely consisted of chores, lawn mowing—whatever his father could drum up.

■ ■ ■

Randy muttered swear words as he dressed in the dark. He heard the front door slam. He knew it was meant to wake him. His father had left the TV on in the kitchen and a half plate of eggs with a sausage link and an empty glass on the counter. The light burned his eyes, so he cut off the overhead and the TV and ate in the dark.

He arrived at the greenhouse in time to help Madison and another man hook a long trailer to a beat-up '70s model Silverado.

"Well, well. Look who's here," Madison shouted from the cab.

"Now who's this young buck?" the other shouted back. He was a tall, stout man, with dark tinted glasses.

Randy wouldn't mind the job too much, but it galled him to be coerced, guilted, or drafted into work.

"Earl's boy," Madison said searching for a trailer pin behind the bench seat. When he found the pin, he threw it to Randy who hooked the trailer to the truck.

"To be sure," he replied. Randy raised the trailer jack. "Don't look near's ugly as Earl. Must take after his mama."

"Maybe the milkman." Madison winked at the man.

"Lois," the man said. "Ol' Lois Lawson. Rolls right off the tongue. Always did."

Randy didn't know how to talk to men his father's age. He searched for anything to say, but Mr. Madison spoke. "This here's my brother Wayne, you know Maggie over there, and that's Polly."

The Madison sister, Maggie, stood outside the greenhouse with Polly, waiting for the trailer. He recognized Maggie from church. She had once been his Sunday school teacher. Polly was a young woman, he guessed his sister's age. When the trailer pulled up, they loaded a couple hundred trays of tobacco plants and left for the fields.

In the truck Randy noticed Wayne had an empty Diet Mountain Dew bottle between his legs. Occasionally he would lift the bottle to his lips and spit chew. The dark tobacco-saliva mixture would slide down the inside of the green bottle leaving messy streaks and a black puddle in the bottom. Randy watched this each time in spite of himself.

"You chew?" he asked.

"No."

"Put hair on your chest."

"No thanks."

"Your pa chew?"

"Nah."

"Course he don't." He stretched his nose and spat in the bottle.

They drove to a large field where the soil had been ridged for tobacco, eight rows between truck middles.

"You done this before ain't ya, Randy?" Mr. Madison asked.

"Nah. I was always in school when dad set tobacco."

"Ain't nothing to it. Maggie and Wayne are going to ride the transplanter. You and Polly follow behind. Put those bigger plants in your buckets, and when they miss a hill or one don't set right, plug a hole with your plant peg and stick one in there. Bury the roots. Got it?"

"Sure."

"Ain't brain surgery, just plant a hill whenever they miss. Watch Polly. She knows what she's doing. Ain't that right, Polly?" he shouted as he climbed the tractor.

"That's right, Mr. Madison."

Polly, a short, round woman with dark skin and bright eyes, laughed after anyone spoke. She wore an old Redskins t-shirt and stone-washed jeans, both stained with tobacco and work. She had on an obliterated pair of classic low-top Reeboks, the kind Randy remembered his grandmother wearing in the '80s.

They filled their buckets while Wayne helped his sister on the transplanter. Madison shouted over the sputtering, "Here we go," and the tractor began.

It was hypnotizing to watch the transplanter work. The riders kept a manic pace, refilling the chambers, pulling plants with the left hand while alternately keeping the right busy dropping plants into the revolving mechanism.

They followed the machine at a leisurely pace. "Well, this isn't so hard," Randy said.

Polly paused. He waited to see why. She pointed five hills behind him with her plant peg. There he spotted a half-set plant he'd overlooked.

"Oh." He pegged a hole, dropped the plant in, and enclosed the ground around it.

"Lordy." She had looked ahead and noticed a gap in her row with five or six missing plants.

"Whoa!" Wayne called from the transplanter already twenty yards away. The tractor stopped. Randy could see Wayne making adjustments to the machine.

When they caught up, Madison shouted, "Y'all catch all them?"

"Sure 'nough," Polly shouted back.

"Polly's sharp; she'll get it done right. You keeping Randy straight, Polly?"

"Yes, sir."

"You *know* Polly don't miss nothing. She's an old pro," Maggie said.

When the tractor reached the end of the row, Madison lifted the transplanter, turned sharply, and settled back down on two new rows. They continued in this fashion replacing the missing hills, exchanging empty trays for full ones, refilling their small buckets as the sun rose on the workers. The work was relentless though not too taxing—even pleasant at times. It was mid-April and still cool in the mornings, only warm early afternoon, a blessing, Randy knew from experience.

He learned quite a lot about Polly. A fellow alum of Southern, graduated four years before his older sister—he was surprised to learn she had three children. She had a young face and a big smile. Only when she stooped to work did her age seem conspicuous, the way she bent over, leaning on her knees, and how she groaned herself upright.

Madison shouted and stopped the tractor. He turned and yelled at Randy, "You see that hill over there?" He pointed, "That one ain't *never* gonna come up."

Randy walked over four rows to where his finger pointed and saw the plant with roots half-exposed to the sunlight. He picked up the plant, dug a new hole, placed it back in the earth and covered the hole.

"Y'all try to keep a better watch, alright?"

"Yes, sir," Randy said.

The tractor began to move again and Polly asked, "How'd you meet him?"

"Goes to my church. I've never really spoke to him, but my dad told him I was looking for work."

"You don't have a job?" she asked.

■ ■ ■

They breaked around nine-thirty. Madison pulled a blue cooler from the back of the Silverado and pointed to Randy. "Drink up."

Randy opened the cooler, letting the lid fall backwards. Immediately its plastic bands snapped. The lid fell backwards ripping its hinges from the cooler and clattering on the truck bed.

"I'll be damned," said Mr. Madison.

"She had two more weeks 'til retirement," Wayne said.

"You treat your daddy's property like that, boy?" Mr. Madison gave Randy an odd look.

"Sorry bout that, sir."

Madison grumbled a kind of acknowledgement and dispersed cans of Wal-Mart brand colas. “No pay today, Polly. Gotta buy a new cooler.”

“Then y’all just leave me at the house come dinner; don’t even come back lookin’ for no help.”

Maggie said, “You wouldn’t leave me alone with this crowd would you, Polly?”

Polly laughed and said, “You can visit any time you want.”

“Get y’all a pack a nabs, too.” Madison passed around a box with peanut butter crackers. “What you doing now, Randy?” he asked. “Your dad tells me you’re thinking about college.”

“Yeah, I thought about college. All my friends are going.” He took a sip. “Tried community last semester, but—”

It was mid-April and still cool in the mornings, only warm early afternoon, a blessing, Randy knew from experience.

“Flunk out?” Wayne asked.

“Nah.” He took a sip of his drink. “Just quit.”

“How come?” Madison asked.

“I don’t know. Felt like a waste of time.”

“Depends on what you want to do,” Maggie said.

“Could do like ol’ Wayne here,” Madison said.

“What’s that?”

“State trooper,” Wayne straightened his back, put his hands on his hips. “Retired.” He spat on the ground.

“Dad says on the Raleigh commute troopers slow traffic down for miles waiting for honest, working folks to make mistakes.”

“That what your old man said?” He spat. “One thing’s for sure, trooper’s the most hated man on the highway.” Wayne recited the superlative with a kind of pride fused with disappointment for all who belittle the plight of the highway patrolman. "Everybody hates a policeman 'til they need one. I say, *You hate a policeman so bad, how bout next time you're in trouble, you ask a damn hippie for help.*"

"A-men," Madison said.

Maggie said, "You could do like your daddy and farm."

"Can't learn that from his daddy no more," Madison said. "Quit farming to be a pill counter, didn't he?"

"I guess."

"Only cotton he's ever gonna pick now's outta a Tylenol bottle," Wayne said. The brothers laughed.

"Well," Madison said, "Farming ain't for some men. It was good enough for my daddy, though—good enough for both your granddaddies, too, as I recall."

The men crushed their cans and tossed them in a bucket. As they walked to the transplanter, they murmured to each other. Randy thought he heard his mother's name. "Hey, Randy," Wayne said. "Your daddy don't ever bring home none of them little blue pills does he?" They laughed like late-night drunks.

"Don't mind them," Maggie said. "Polly knows better, don't she?"

Polly groaned and hopped off the tailgate.

■ ■ ■

Over dinner his father complained about a shift meeting at the plant. Randy's attention trailed in and out between his father and *Jeopardy*. He picked at a piece of fried chicken.

"I'm sorry you did not phrase your answer in the form of a question," he heard Alex say.

"What a stupid rule," Randy said.

"How's the job been?" his father asked.

Randy suddenly felt the impulse to share how the Madisons spoke of both of them. What had they said that angered him so? He tried to recall, but it wasn't the words so much.

"Fine," he bit into a chicken leg.

"How much longer will it take to set his crop?"

"Probably before two weeks."

"Dang. Y'all are moving right along, ain't ya?"

"Yep."

"You like that?"

"It's not bad," Randy said.

His father continued about the shift meeting. Randy watched his mother listen. *How can she?* he thought. *It's not bad enough to work a boring, miserable job—he has to come home and talk about it, make us miserable, and if he ain't talking about his job, he's talking about finding one for me. That's all there is: jobs and talking about jobs. Work. Work and complain. Everybody works so everybody can share the joy of complaining.*

■ ■ ■

Polly and Randy spent their days talking about people they knew, football, music, and daytime television only the elderly, the stay-at-home moms, and the unemployed watched.

"*Judge Mathis*. 'Tough love in the courtroom,'" he said to Polly, and she laughed so hard Madison could hear above the tractor.

"Y'all working or shuckin' and jivin'?" he yelled back.

"Tough love in the courtroom," Polly repeated.

They laughed quietly.

"Shucking and jiving? What the hell does that mean?" Randy asked. "Maybe that's our work names. I'll be 'Shuckin' and you be 'Jivin.'" Randomly Polly would instigate a call and response joke with their new names or announce "tough love in the courtroom," and laugh as the two walked over hundreds of tobacco hills. "You *crazy*, boy." Madison seemed increasingly surly each day, but he never mentioned why.

Randy liked to hear about Polly's family. She and her three children lived with her mother, sister, and cousin, Charlene, and sometimes Charlene's boyfriend. She rolled her eyes whenever she spoke of Charlene.

"Charlene's a pure mess. The man she's hangin' out with—ain't nothing to him neither."

"She got a job?"

"*Naw*, she ain't got *no* job. Well that's not true. Just can't *keep* a job. Likes to sleep too much. Bout like my boyfriend."

"Yeah?"

"I reckon he's my boyfriend. He's always over at the house anyway. Getting sorry like Charlene."

"Why's that?"

"Drinks too much. Got a *good* job. He works at Ballard's Body Shop. Does stuff on his own, too." Polly grunted slightly between sentences. Late in the afternoons, her feet began hurting, so she would walk the fields in her socks. "Sometimes I help him install new windshields. Sometimes I do the work myself while he lays around the house with Charlene." Her smile slipped. "Sometimes I think he spends a little *too* much time with her. She's rubbing off on him." Suddenly she appeared much older than he'd first observed.

"Y'all talkin' or workin'?" Madison shouted.

Polly stooped to replant a hill that didn't need re-setting and grumbled. Randy followed suit. It became easier to miss plants after watching hundreds every day. A thousand plants later, Polly said, "Talk to me or I'mma fall asleep."

■ ■ ■

A cold front was coming. Madison worried a frost could stunt the tender plants creating back-breaking work for the remainder of the growing season.

After church one evening, Randy's father mentioned running into Madison. "Mr. Madison says his stand ain't looking too good."

"Really?"

"You listening to him all right?"

"Yeah, dad. Not much to it. Walk all day, dig a hole, drop in a plant, you're done. What's he saying?"

"Well, he says his stand's looking poor. Seems to think maybe you and Polly aren't catching everything. It's an important job, Randy. You miss too many, it eats the profits. You gotta have a good crew to set. That's one of the most important jobs."

"How on earth could I be screwing up this job? If I can't work in a tobacco field, then what the hell can I do?"

"Just *listen* to the man."

Lying on the couch that night with his eyes closed, Randy could see tobacco plants ever-dropping, soft soil, tractor tires turning and churning, lumbering Polly, imitation Coke, and peanut butter crackers.

"Still up for breakfast?" his father asked on his way to bed.

"Sure."

"Why don't you get up a little earlier and eat with me for a change?"

Randy didn't answer.

"Or don't. Your choice."

"Night."

Monday the cold front settled in—no frost, but a constant fog and a chilly mist. Madison was keeping a closer watch on Polly and Randy's work.

"My knees hurt, and my ankles hurt," Polly said. "This weather's bad for 'em. Be glad when we're done. You gonna help Mr. Madison this summer?"

"Hope not."

Polly laughed. "Oughta go back to school."

Randy glanced over a few rows to a sliver of rock, a hard white edge in the dark soil. He knelt and stuck his finger in the ground beneath the rock and it fell into his hand. He smiled as he wiped the stone clean with his thumb.

"What you got there?" Polly asked.

"An arrowhead," he said. Almost as long as his pinky finger, a perfect isosceles triangle with two wing tip notches at the bottom. The edges were still sharp and minutely serrated like a shark's tooth. "I can't wait to show this to my dad. He's got a couple boxes full of these, not half as perfect as this one."

"What y'all doin' back there?" They heard Madison yell down the row.

Randy glanced over a few rows to a sliver of rock, a hard white edge in the dark soil. He knelt and stuck his finger in the ground beneath the rock and it fell into his hand.

They resumed walking to catch up, glancing for the missing hills, resetting a few here and there. As the tractor turned at the end, Madison watched Randy hastily dart his plant peg in the ground, drop in a plant, and pat the dirt.

"Hold on," he shouted. He parked and hopped off. "You see that one you just set there?"

"Yeah."

"That ain't worth a *damn*."

Polly looked away with the sheepish look of a scolded child.

"You ain't patting the soil down worth a *damn*. If you don't angle it right, you leave a pocket of air by the roots. It won't live. Some of ‘em might, but most of ‘em won’t. Didn’t you know that?”

“I don’t know.”

“Damn it all. No wonder my crop’s looking like shit everywhere I go. Dead plants everywhere I look.” His brother and sister tried to busy themselves.

“Sorry.”

Madison grunted. “Y’all tighten up. We ain’t got much more to go. I don’t want us to have to walk back over all we done and re-set by hand, but by God, if y’all keep screwing around we’ll have to.”

He climbed the tractor and started again.

“Yeah, and he’ll pay me for *that,* too,” Polly said.

Randy looked at Polly.

“And I’ll be shuckin’ and jivin’ all the way to the bank,” she said.

All Randy’s anger disappeared. He laughed silently with Polly. *Madison needs me,* Randy thought, and the idea seemed so funny. *This asshole needs me,* and suddenly being a worker didn’t seem so bad. He liked walking, talking with Polly, and the arrowhead easily erased at least a dozen wrongs. In the fields there’d been plenty of space and time enough to think. He contemplated the material he’d studied in World History and literature, Karl Marx, the class struggles, the perils of the worker, and the injustices instilled by the owning class. He thought about Dickens—simple, happy “Joe Gargery,” beating and clanging as a smith, and the ever-wretched “Pip,” feebly struggling up his social ladder. He had thoughts like: the man who owns nothing is freer than any Carnegie or Rockefeller. He thought about Thoreau alone in his Walden cabin. He thought about how the Native Americans must have lived before the settlers. No money. A world where work improved everyone’s lives rather than destroyed them. He felt the arrowhead in his pocket. This is mine, he thought—all that I can see and feel and know—and I don't need their wealth. I won't waste my life on work.

"Polly, I'm glad I ain't gotta run around and look for guys like me to help make my living, help save the farm. I'd sure hate to know it all depended on a community college dropout." He knelt to re-set a plant.

"I didn't think you'd still be squatting down like that at the end of all this, but I'll be danged if you ain't."

"You barely bend your back." He did an over-exaggerated imitation of Polly setting a plant with the least motion possible, all arms and back, no legs or knees.

"Get on, you and your young back."

They took a late break around ten. Madison seemed to begrudge them colas and peanut butter crackers. When Randy finished, he shoved his hand into his pocket. He had a compulsive fear the arrowhead was missing. Since the discovery he'd found it harder to keep his eyes on the rows. Any odd-looking stone might be another. He held the white arrowhead to his chest and ran his thumb once more across the sharp edge. He thought how easily it might draw blood even after hundreds of years—how fascinating to think of the craftsmanship. Something that lasts for hundreds of years. How was it made? Did a man or a young boy craft this? He imagined the stone fixed to an arrow, hurtling through the air, piercing its target. A deer maybe. Did it ever kill? He raised his find between two fingers. Its tapered edges glinted translucent in the sun.

With a quick motion, Madison snatched the arrowhead from his hand.

"*This* what I'm paying you to do?"

Randy looked at Madison. "No, sir."

"Seems like I been paying you to look for rocks. That's what I been doing." He tossed the arrowhead up and down in his hand twice.

Randy kept silent, his stare fixed on Madison.

Madison placed his index finger along the edge as if he were going to skip it across a pond and flung the stone with a sidearm throw over the rows of tobacco, towards the edge of the woods.

■ ■ ■

The work lasted three more days after which Randy was paid for his time. He said nothing when Madison thanked him for his work. The check felt flimsy, worthless in his hand. Madison's gratitude was the obligatory kind cashiers dole out at grocery store checkout lanes, like bank teller smiles and waitress goodnights. He'd done the work; he deserved the money. A piece of paper with the signature of a man for whom he felt no respect—this is what it's all about, he thought. This is what work is.

He cashed the piece of paper the next day and resolved not to look back.

But he liked Polly, and he liked being outdoors, the cool, early-spring mornings, and the clean weariness he felt at the end of each day. He wouldn't forget these. But Madison and his anger left him stewing in bitter hatred, not for Madison and his actions, but hatred for his very own life—exchanging his life for wages, hatred for his own worthless future and the meaningless jobs, the emptiness of work that becomes the substance of life.

■ ■ ■

The following Sunday, the cold front had moved along, and the May warmth arrived. At dinner Randy seemed uneasy. Later he sat on the couch like a patient in a waiting room, his father in his chair with the paper folded, un-read in his hands. "Want to go for a ride?" he asked.

"Yeah."

They began driving to town in the old farm truck, a rusted, yellow vehicle, rarely driven now. Randy ran his hand along the bench seat's ripped leather. He remembered the first time his father let him drive. Without a word, his father had parked and got out of the truck. He grinned as he opened the passenger door. "Slide over," he said. Randy needed no instruction. He'd driven tractors for years. This was simpler. No clutch, high or low gears, no right and left brakes: just gas and brake. "You're off the path," his father said in the memory, and he recalled the tractor's main advantage—the field of vision. Just open air and a horizon of land.

Now, Randy could feel his dad preparing to turn left into a neighborhood. "Keep straight," he said. After a few turns they were several miles from town, driving countryside neither frequented.

"It's odd how unfamiliar your hometown can feel. Three roads out of your way can look like another state if you never drive them once in awhile."

Randy nodded.

"Where we going?" his father asked.

"Farther."

They drove ten minutes more. "There," Randy said. "Up that path."

He slowed the truck. "We don't know whose land that is. Probably shouldn't."

"Then stop the truck. Pull off the road here. I'll walk."

"I don't think you should, Randy."

"If you don't, I'm going to drive mom's car here when we get home."

"Alright." His father pulled over. Randy got out and slammed the door. "Where you going, son?"

His father caught up beside him. Randy was scanning the edge of the forest, looking over Madison's land. They walked down two adjacent rows. The plants were thriving and had turned a darker shade. Evenly spaced, row after row, they dotted the entire field, precisely laid in their pale green grid.

"I don't know what Mr. Madison was talking about; he's got a great stand, here. There's barely a hill missing in the whole dang field. Always thought he was a mite curious."

Randy kept his eyes on the forest beyond the field.

"I know a lot of farmers like that, you know? Nothing ever suits them. Always see the worst in a crop. Worry themselves to death about it 'til it's harvested and sold. You know, there's *curious*, and then there's *damn foolish*. Yes, sir. He's got a good stand."

"Dad, do you like working at the plant?"

"The plant? It's not so bad. It's a job."

They reached the edge of the woods. Randy began kicking around in the overgrowth.

"Don't you sometimes wish we were still farming?"

The plants were thriving and had turned a darker shade. Evenly spaced, row after row, they dotted the entire field, precisely laid in their pale green grid.

"Some days. Some days I miss it like crazy. The outdoors, no meetings, no management over your shoulder." He took a deep breath and let it out slowly. "How about you?"

"Sometimes," his son answered.

"What are we here for?"

"Hold on." With his back to the woods, Randy aimed his finger at the corner of the field and counted. At eight, he walked to where his finger landed.

"Counting rows?"

"Truck middles."

At the eighth truck middle, near the field's edge, Randy observed the tree trunks, any peculiar branches, tall weeds, or brush. Then he noticed a young dogwood with faded blooms. His dad followed him to the tree.

"I hate that you and mom have to work."

His father laughed. "That's life, buddy. Everybody's gotta work."

"I know. I just hate y'all do. I hate that y'all gotta help put me through school and help me pay for a car and feed me and—"

"That's what we're *supposed* to do, Randy."

"I guess."

A few minutes passed with rustling of grass and fallen leaves.

Finally, Randy said: "I hate people tell you what to do, and you have to listen."

"At the plant?"

"Yeah. I hate somebody your age or even younger tells you what to do."

"Well, if you wanna know the truth, I ain't crazy about it either." He looked across the field. "That's what I liked most about farming. When you got down to it, end of the day, it was just you, the land, and whatever hand God dealt you."

Randy walked to the dogwood again, and turned around and walked ten feet away. Then, from a slightly different angle, he returned to the tree. He repeated this pattern until he'd scoured much of the area within a ten-foot radius of the tree, always returning.

"If Mr. Madison said or did something that offended you, you should probably let me know. I'll talk to him. But there's no sense bottling it up. Ain't good for you, and it ain't good—"

"Found it." Randy uncovered the arrowhead with the toe of

his shoe. He snatched it off the ground and squeezed it in his hand until its sharpened edges nearly broke the skin.

"What you got?"

He placed it in his father's palm.

"Hey! Danged if that ain't a beauty—pretty near perfect. I haven't found one of these in years." He ran his thumb on the smooth, flat surface and laughed. "Used to make my day when I'd find one," he said.

At home, Randy's father produced three cigar boxes of carved stones, spear points, pottery fragments, and arrowheads from the bottom of his gun cabinet and set them on the dining room table. Randy examined one after the other with wonder, admiring their distinct beauty, each unique, he imagined, as the hands that fashioned them.

"What you gonna do with all these?" he asked.

"Not sure. Guess I should put them in a display case so people could see and handle 'em." He picked up an arrowhead made of a pale green stone and shaped like an almond. "My granddaddy broke a lot of the land that we used to tend. Daddy said when he'd plow the fields above the house here, he'd see so many of them he wouldn't get off the tractor to pick them up. Said he'd never get anything done."

Randy pictured his grandfather in the old model B John Deere, harrowing the land and turning up arrowheads like tender pale potatoes.

He held an arrowhead fashioned from pure quartz to the light—the centerpiece of his father's collection. He closed one eye and looked through the stone as if it were a lens. The crystalline rock looked like it might melt away to touch.

"A civilization of people, and all that's left behind are their tools."

"All the work we do, dad, and what will we leave behind? Anything as perfect as this?"

They placed the artifacts back in their boxes. "You asked me what I should do with them," his father said. "I've often wondered myself. Maybe I'd never do it, but I think before I die, I ought to go out to the fields we tended, and the woods we rambled and hunted—all our favorite places—spread them out everywhere, back to the land." Randy imagined the arrowheads returned, scattered and buried in the earth like seeds: silent stones waiting undiscovered for another hundred, two hundred years. "Ain't hardly right to keep all that joy to yourself, huh?" his father said. "Then, one day when we're long gone, somebody like you and me will discover one of these beauties; they'll feel lucky, won't they? Like for once in their life, they were right where they were meant to be." ■

I SAW BOBBY BARE KISS MARTY STUART

on the stage of the Ryman after Bobby had played *Marie Laveau*
and *That's How I Got to Memphis* and *Detroit City* and my friend

who's a music manager whispered to me that Bobby Bare
was the sweetest man in Nashville and his voice was pitch perfect

at age 78 and he still wore washed out jeans and a white hat and a sloppy
overshirt and no shit or horsing around on stage just straight ahead music

so that by the time it was over and he kissed Marty Stuart goodbye
I was crying but I was on the verge anyway being at the Ryman where

my parents stopped on their honeymoon one October night in 1952
and saw Ernest Tubb and Little Jimmy Dickens and Minnie Pearl

and I didn't know the Ryman stage was so small but The Grand Ole Opry
Square Dancers have just clogged in a corner of that little stage in their red

checkered outfits and white tap shoes and I felt the same homesickness
I felt the first time I saw *Coal Miner's Daughter* and Ted says to Clary

Get up Mommy do your Squaw Dance and she does and I'm the only one
in the theatre weeping at what most people thought was hokey and hillbilly

but it made me miss the old TV shows that broadcast into my father's
den every Saturday afternoon and we all quit what we were doing

to watch Lester & Earl and Teddy & Doyle & Loretta and Porter
& Pretty Miss Norma Jean & later Dolly and my daddy would holler

into the kitchen for my mother to come out to the den and look here
at Ole Possum or Charley Pride or Wilma Lee and Stoney Cooper

singing *Walking My Lord Up Calvary's Hill* and when the credits rolled
on the *Wilburn Brothers Show* Loretta would kick off her shoes

and dance that Squaw Dance in her stocking feet and I tell you I lived
for that on Saturdays until one time in 1973 Daddy stood up from his

TV watching chair and yelled for all of us to come running
quick and watch this little feller picking the mandolin with Lester

Flatt's new band on Porter Wagoner's show and we grouped
around the Zenith and gaped at Marty Stuart's wizardry and I fell dead

in love with him that very moment and now here we are 40 years later
and he's reinvented that template of old country music TV shows

with an opening hit, a comic, a guest or two, the girl singer, and hymn
time and invites all his old friends and shepherds the young unknowns

the way Lester still shepherds him and they all play at his annual late
night jam and this year fireworks blazed above the Ryman before we went

into the show and Marty stood on stage three straight hours in his black
frock coat nodding his wild shock of hair back and forth and tapping

his boot and then he brought out his mommy and made her tell all about
her new book of photographs and before we knew it the Mavericks

were burning down the house with *All You Ever Do Is Bring Me Down*
then Marty asks Raul Malo to sing a birthday song to Manuel the glitter

tailor who is also on stage because Marty honors all parts of country
music even costumes and Raul sings Don Gibson's *I'd Be a Legend*

in My Time and I cry even harder because once when I was a kid we saw
Don Gibson in the K-Mart when he lived in Knoxville in a beat up trailer

on Clinton Highway and had seen better days but Mother had all his records
and then when I think I can't cry any more Marty says they are all going

upstairs after the show to shake and howdy with anyone who wants
to meet them and have their picture made and sometimes it's 4 a.m.

before they can leave the Ryman but I am too embarrassed to admit how
much I love Marty and his wife Connie Smith and now Hilda his mommy

and don't want to make a fan fool of myself so we step out into the late
night and watch the crowd leave and listen to people converse

in German and Spanish and maybe Bengali and I realize they too love
this exceptionally long musical that crosses decades and languages

and has carried us to Nashville where the noisy streets are still teeming
with girls in Western boots and boys in Western shirts and music blares

out of every bar we pass on Broadway and lifts us into the cacophony
and even when we get back home and even now I can't stop crying

MARIANNE WORTHINGTON

THE MOUNTAINEER'S DAUGHTER

Bathed in red spotlights,
the color of cheap wine,
the girl in the print dress smiles.
Her voice, high and clear
as mountain air,
almost unheard in the noisy room.

Truck drivers swill their beer,
laugh at old jokes
only seeing breasts and legs,
not slender hands
or sad dark eyes
that cut through the smoky gloom.

Songs become twisting roads,
highways of country regrets
that lead away to city streets.
In a metal cry of guitars

the present place dissolves
and banjos levitate above clouds.

Rocking chairs fly like bats
through a grandmothers dreams
and change, as chords transpose,
to sparrows.

BRADLEY R. STRAHAN

LISTENING TO A RECORDING OF EDDEN HAMMONS PLAYING "GENERAL WASHINGTON'S MARCH"

The guitarist is clearly out of his depth,
adequate, sure – skilled even – but he isn't
standing on the same earth as the fiddler,
and the fiddler isn't standing on the earth

at all: with each pass through the tune
he floats another millimeter above the ground
so that the flattened grass springs back
beneath his feet and begins, again, to grow.

He never plays it the same way twice,
not even once, his variations seemingly infinite
and almost magical, the way the low light can turn
a hillside from fallow to fire some summer evenings

or how the glassy river is the same river
when it goes dull under the wind’s flat hand,
and returns stranger when, in sudden calm,
it snaps back to placid glass.

DOUG VAN GUNDY

BLACK RADIO

It was a Zenith Trans-Oceanic, with rows of red-orange push buttons
and serial black tuning knobs that said the path to Wonder commenced
with a frequency indicator floating like the bubble in a carpenter's level.
My father listened to WSM, the Grand Ole Opry, on Saturday nights,
drifting to sleep to Hank Snow or Roy Acuff or a bluegrass band
he could tell you the history of. Sleepwear consisted of a t-shirt
and J.C. Penney pajama bottoms. When he and my mother yet
slept together, she would be awake be on her side of the bed—
propped up and reading, an L & M burning in a crystal ashtray.
Telling him *Turn it down!* until the singer's voice was a whisper.
Whatever happens when we die, suffering will have to be explained.
Maybe God will pass out the Trans-Oceanics, and the dead will huddle
around the nearest set, listening to Heaven's version of a fireside chat.
Maybe she'll find him—my father—and they'll argue about the volume.
Despite all the hoakum I like to think there's more than breathlessness
and the tumult reduced to sleep in a dark so total you'd want a radio.
I like to think we'd have hands to tune the notched knobs. Eyes to judge
where the Nashville station is clearest and the voices of hearts absolve us

and death is a song we automatically sing, knowing nearly all the words.
Maybe we're dead and the trespass of living rises like so much smoke.

ROY BENTLEY

THAT BOY FROM THE '50S

I've seen him sitting at a small table
in that rose and aqua kitchen
at the row of windows farthest from the stove
coloring in his Peter Pan book while his mother cooks
and hums along with Patti Page or The McGuire Sisters.

Sometimes he's falling asleep in his room
as if on a boat rocking gently
on the ebb and flow of his parents' bridge club,
an exotic burnished horizon
beneath the door down the long dark hall
from which floats the odd oracular word—
Ike, Adlai, Hitchcock, Khrushchev—
on magic waves of muted laughter,
clucks and murmurs, Chesterfields,
Folgers, and White Shoulders.

And I want to reach down for this boy

and scoop him up and carry him away
before he's seduced by the era's mounting desperation
for conformity, for keeping up with the Joneses,
for winning friends and influencing people,
and by its fears—of Communism
and The Bomb, Desegregation, Outer Space.

But where in the world would I presume to take him,
in this world that's burning beyond anything
we could ever have imagined?

He's only recently appeared with such clarity,
usually when I wake in the middle of the night.
Unbidden by any dream or song cue
this child appears—you appear—
across the decades, just as clearly as can be.
What a surprise and how grateful I am.
If I'd known, I'd have run to the store
and looked for Baby Ruths
or some of those Sky Blue Popsicles you like.

I like seeing you in that time and place
of such insistent harmony
between the storms, that world which
the McGuires and Patti and Doris and Rosie sang sincerely,
with its coins in the fountain seeking happiness,
and the moon hitting our eyes like big pizza pies,
and even when someone was sad it was
a beautiful sort of sadness
about remembering a night
and a waltz in Tennessee—
so many pretty ladies hoping
that we may always be a dreamer
and may our wildest dreams come true.

I wouldn’t dream of telling you
you haven’t turned out
quite as I might have hoped—
and somehow I believe
you’ll return the favor.
Seeing you so clearly now

gives me the chance to tell you
it wasn't your fault
that you lost innocence along the way.
It's not something we misplace
like our Davy Crockett cap
or the left ear for Mr. Potato Head—
it gets nibbled away,
and not by the Godzillas and the Gorgos
but by the everyday monsters of the world.
We seem now to have learned so much,
but to what avail?

Here, take my hand,
and—as Patti admonished—
we'll leave our fickle past behind us
and cross over that bridge.

I can't thank you enough for looking me up.
We can't relearn the innocence,
but I appreciate your coming back to remind me—

now, when it seems especially useful—
that when we do not know any better
there is nothing to fear.

So, let's always be a dreamer
and may our wildest dreams come true.

HADLEY HURY

HOLLER

JAD ADKINS

I was walking to a friend's house one evening along one of the few roads that jam here every Friday as people leave town, when a woman leaning out of a pickup truck stopped at the light and saw me and hollered, *Where's the closest bar or hotel?* I turned and smiled, thinking she'd seen me walking and thought I looked tired and just wanted to remind me *it's the weekend, baby, it's 5 o'clock somewhere.* She was middle-aged and overweight and I could see she was struggling to hold herself up and out the window, which might explain her impatience in having to repeat the question, but the closer I got to the truck the more clearly I saw the panic in her eyes, that there was no lightheartedness in her asking, that this was not some end-of-the-work-week banter quipped one tired soul to another but the voice of someone with need deeper than thirst or sleep. Taste: unlimited. The closest bar. The closest hotel.

I pointed and told her two blocks and she said thank you and sped off and immediately I knew—even wanted—what she wanted, how sometimes when I'm driving through small town USA I feel the same special desperation to duck into the darkest hole-in-the-wall bar or economy motel room, something soaked in chain smoke and cherry air-freshener, smells I both love and hate and associate with West Virginia, the hometown I see in every particle board drawer Gideon Bible and throwback neon sign whining It's Miller Time. I'm not drawn to these places by drink or the need to sleep it off but by an inner barfly buzzed on coal dust and a smokestack and a Mountain Dew bottle sticky with sugar spit and Skoal, that every time I pull a foldout chair up to a warped woodprint laminate table I feel like a home come prodigal son sorry for ever leaving. That I could stare at the menthols mashed in an ashtray for hours and dream of ponds, could wrap myself up in a cheap flower-print comforter and think of my grandmother Mae, who I haven't hugged in ten years, who always smelled delightfully like the cold dirt basement where she used to wash her aprons. Somehow I think if I'd hitched a ride in the back of that pick up it would've taken me to her and all my other distant relatives living out Lincoln County, out in the country, those dark hollers I'm drawn to and dread all at once, how I'm ashamed of them, how I resent the dead beat of the Ten Mile heart in me, the poverty of my blood, the shotgun and the four wheeler and the gas station room temp fried chicken I can't get enough of. Somehow I think if I'd squeezed into the cab beside her I'd recognize the same hard look I see on faces of old friends who've never left West Virginia and never will, those stuck working six tens at the refinery, one shift away from that big breakthrough or breakdown, whose off days are wasted in camouflage Carhartt codeine purple stupors playing online hold'em or the slots always just one more spin from redemption. I miss them all dearly when I'm away and avoid them when I'm in, those faces that get thinner and thinner with every friend God calls home found dead in his apartment; those faces that bear witness to every funeral I've been out of town for. I hear them calling out to me from the VFW and the K K with the question where have you been?—and it makes me homesick to think our bodies belong on barstools, that when they finally open us up we'll smell of summer tar, our lungs the color of the water-stained ceiling tiles we know by heart.

So where is the closest bar or hotel? Where can I find that free-HBO-blue-motel-window light that will lead me back to the house I grew up in, take me back to the town smothered by chemical and coal and the factory whir I can't sleep without? Who has a room with walls thin enough that I might hear the raspy voices next door and be reminded of the distant great aunts I've never met in faraway hollers where my blood comes from and runs like littered creek water carrying the stink of algae and crawdads and the good cold mud from which I'm made. ■

BOOK REVIEW

Ann Pancake. ***Me and My Daddy Listen to Bob Marley: Novellas and Stories.*** **Berkeley, Ca.: Counterpoint Press, 2015. 289 pages. Hardcover. $24.00.**

Reviewed by Elaine Fowler Palencia

In the lead story of Ann Pancake's compelling new collection, a novella called "In Such Light," Janie is spending the summer back with her grandparents in Remington, West Virginia, convalescing from "running herself down" in college. She works part-time as a popcorn girl at the Alexander Henry movie theater; hangs out with Uncle Bobby, who has mental disabilities; gets involved with Nathan, a slacker neighbor; and searches for herself and for her place in the community. This set-up employs a number of Pancake hallmarks: a worn-down multi-generational family situation;

a fog of poverty and bad decision-making; the complicated relationship of the main character to rural West Virginia; the lives of people with mental disabilities and/or mental illness in small communities; and a journey towards epiphany.

The struggle of the people and mountains of West Virginia to recover from the depredations of extractive industries forms the backdrop of this collection. In "Arsonists," Dell and his childhood friend Kenny hold out in abandoned Tout, West Virginia, watching over the few houses left after the mountaintops have been removed by the same mix of ammonium nitrate and fuel oil that Timothy McVeigh used in Oklahoma City. The description is merciless:

> *Six months into that gray blizzard, the company started offering the buyouts. By then, a lot of the properties were good and blast-busted, with walls cracked, ceilings dropping, foundations split. Wells knocked dry. By the time the offers came, the homeowners had been told by the Department of Environmental Protection that they couldn't prove the damage hadn't been there before the blasting started, and no one had the lawyer money to argue with them, so many people sold, even at the pathetic prices offered them. If their houses weren't shot, their nerves were, and those who could start over, did.*

Someone starts torching the abandoned properties. Dell's wife gets cancer. Kenny loses his mind. But Dell and Kenny cannot abandon the ruined land they love. No winners here, except, as usual, big money.

An equally disturbing story, certainly to dog lovers, is "Dog Song." Matley, a marginal figure, has an abiding love for the twenty-three dogs he lives with, and through them a profound connection to his humanity. The dogs start disappearing.

Who is taking them? Is it the Oaken Acre Estates people, who have built fancy homes nearby and want to clean up the area? Is it the "train people," who run a sightseeing train through the mountains so tourists can enjoy Appalachia without touching it? Is it the outcast, Johnby, who may or may not be dangerous? After Matley learns what happened to his dogs, he begins to lose his place in time and his sense of identity, except as he is viewed by strangers on a train: " ... and he understands he is blighted landscape. He is disruption of scenery. Understands he is the last one left, and nothing but a sight. A sight." This is a bitter view of innocence dispossessed, of Eden lost.

The original voice that astonished readers in Pancake's first collection...is here more refined...

A number of stories employ totems to carry a sense of mystery and of another world hovering behind this one. In "Mousekull," a girl wears a death-redolent mouse skull around her neck as she circles the fact of her grandfather's suicide. In "The Knowing," a woman who moved away returns to roam the hills, drawn by a "knowing" that leads her to animal bones. "What did it mean always to find bone at the end?" She tries, using paradox—"grounded rapture," "weightless presence, "uncharged euphoria"—to express the moment that T.S. Eliot called "the still, turning point:" It is a longed-for feeling of enlightenment, of understanding that "I didn't end with my skin."

The title story turns on paradox as well, the heartbreaking triumph of Mish, three, who cannot speak clearly and is at the mercy of his selfish father. Mish is sustained by three things: his Dallas Cowboys jacket, a clutch of action figures, and the music of Bob Marley, played when he and his father are in the car and are thus between disasters. Fury at his father's exploitation of him after the jacket disappears, probably in a drug trade, finally gives Mish the power of comprehensible speech, which the loser father fears. Because even a three-year-old can see the world more clearly than a substance-abusing man who is looking through a pair of contact lenses he stole from his own mother.

The original voice that astonished readers in Pancake's first collection, *Given Ground*, is here more refined, surer, and even more distinctive. Nobody else has this eye for the dark places where hard truths hide. Nobody else could have written these eleven stories.

Cat Pleska. *Riding on Comets: A Memoir*. Morgantown, W.Va.: Vandalia Press, 2015. 236 pages. Softcover. $16.99.

Reviewed by Donna M. Crow

If Cat Pleska is riding on comets, her family members are the constellations she observes on her journey. Descriptions of her father's drinking, her mother's depression, hospitalization and electroshock therapy, are juxtaposed against Christmas memories, playing I Spy with Mom, learning about the stars with her dad, and listening to stories at the heels of her grandparents, all seemingly without judgment or interpretation.

Pleska heralds the mundane with a vivid memory, spoken in the voices of her people with stories that repeat themselves in every generation until it's impossible to discern whether the author lived them or simply inherited them like the color of her hair.

Assembled within sections entitled "Images," "Awakening," "Awareness," "Reaction," and "Loss," and "Strength," these short, easy-to-read essays compile a family photo album whose pictures are angled from the lens of an only child living among adults.

The first thirty-eight pages, comprised of seven chapters, are micro-snapshots more than complete essays—some are only one or two pages in length). While we might long for more direction as to where we are headed, these snippets allow the reader to glimpse the sights, smells, and sounds of Pleska's world from her youngest memories.

Pleska's scenes are full of sensory details that turn her specifics into the universal experience of an everyday rural American upbringing:

> *Peddling fast against the dark, I'd fly home to smells of meatloaf and freshly made biscuits. After dinner was television,* I Love Lucy *or* Flintstones. *Our front door faced west, and I remember standing to watch the sun set between the huge maple and oak trees across the street.*

In chapter seven, "In Mommaw's Kitchen", we sit alongside the young narrator as she overhears her mother and Aunt discuss a visit from a government worker, possibly a tax assessor. One woman is fixing the other's hair while our narrator schemes how to get another cookie from the kitchen. "Asked me a buncha questions. I remember Warren talked to one of them afore, not long after we was married. Anyhow, he was at work when this little feller showed up." The scene isn't spectacular for its drama and may not move the story forward, but it serves an auditory purpose. Pleska's attention to dialect and syntax is spot on, allowing us to hear what she heard and providing little peepholes into the ordinary Appalachian American life.

As the narrator becomes more sophisticated, so does the writing. It is not until the section entitled "Awakening" that we start to see the narrator's internal processes, though ever so diplomatic.

In chapter ten, "Night Light," the opening passage begins as innocent as the narrator herself, yet we know something is amiss: "Little white missiles from dandelion blossoms floated through the air and past my head as I pulled my red wagon toward the edge of my grandparents' backyard." Mention of the blossoms sounds harmless, yet they are missiles which intend to plant themselves and spread, causing destruction to a beautiful lawn. And while a red wagon is staple for many a childhood and possibly a symbol of innocence, red is also the color of danger. She is pulling her red wagon to the edge of her grandparents' yard where some amount of her innocence will be lost. She is on the edge. Destruction awaits.

In this scene, although she recognizes that tent caterpillars are damaging the apple tree, she attempts to collect them and set them free, saving them from her grandparents' torch. Her mind is still separate from the people whose actions no doubt influence her own. Then, as dark ensues, she begins collecting fireflies in a jar to later light the dark night of her room. As she lurks in the shadows of the yard with her "night light," a fight breaks out between her grandfather and an uncle who she refers to as "dark shapes" or "giants." Both had been drinking heavily. While trying to break up the fight her grandmother gets struck, grunts, and storms inside and off to bed to also become a "dark shape." Standing in the shadows, she is still set apart from the "dark shapes" which are supposed to be keeping her safe. The girl has witnessed everything from the whiskey intake to fisticuffs to the slamming of doors, all the while attempting to collect little shards of light from the night air. After it is all over, she makes her way to bed by herself, with no comforting words from adults.

Pleska's lack of emotion makes us believe this sort of commotion is commonplace, yet she is distracted enough that she forgets to punch air holes in the jar lid for the "lightning bugs." The essay ends when she wakes the next morning to find them as "they lay still at the bottom of the jar. Their glow was gone." This single, telling detail denotes a loss of innocence and becomes a sort of turning point in the memoir as the narrator becomes part of the human landscape of joy and suffering that encases her.

By the end of the last section, "Strength", we understand that it takes a certain amount of fortitude to simply live, and that wisdom comes from every day experience such as when the grandmother, while peeling bruised apples for canning, simply says, "There's always bad parts. Got the good with the bad. Just the way it is."

This memoir is not heavy-handed in that the author does not revel in her insights, nor does she lament her grievances. But this is a double-edged sword. While we don't want a memoir to be whiny, at times, the essays feel almost numb, and the reader is left wanting a deeper connection with the narrator. ■

CONTRIBUTORS

Jad Adkins is a recent graduate of Georgia College's MFA program. His essays have appeared or are forthcoming in *Fourth Genre, The Pinch, South Loop Review, Sonora Review, Jelly Bucket,* and elsewhere. He is currently the nonfiction editor of *Pinball.*

Darnell Arnoult is the writer-in-residence and co-director of the Mountain Heritage Literary Festival at Lincoln Memorial University in Harrogate, Tennessee. She is also co-editor of the literary magazine *Drafthorse.* Arnoult is the prize-winning author of *What Travels With Us: Poems* (LSU Press) and the novel *Sufficient Grace* (Free Press). Her work has appeared in *Appalachian Heritage, Asheville Poetry Review, Nantahala Review,* and *Southwest Review.*

Roy Bentley has published nine chapbooks and three books of poetry, including *The Trouble with a Short Horse in Montana* and *Starlight Taxi.* His poems have appeared in the *Southern Review, North American Review, Prairie Schooner, Shenandoah, Blackbird, Sou'wester, American Literary Review,* and elsewhere. He has received awards and fellowships from the National Endowment for the Arts, the Florida Division of Cultural Affairs, and the Ohio Arts Council.

Christie Collins is a doctoral student studying Literature and Creative Writing at the University of Louisiana-Lafayette. Additionally, she teaches full-time in the Department of English at LSU. Her poems have recently appeared in *Cold Mountain Review, Reunion: The Dallas Review, Wicked Alice, So to Speak, Still: The Journal,* and *Canyon Voices.* Her chapbook titled *Along the Diminishing Stretch of Memory* is available through Dancing Girl Press.

Jackson Connor lives and writes in southeast Ohio with his spouse and four kids. He earned an MFA from the University of Utah and a PhD from Ohio University. His essay "Rara Avis" was a notable in *Best American Essays,* and his recent work has appeared in *AGNI, River Teeth,* and *Stealing Time.*

Donna M. Crow lives in Irvine, Kentucky, on her family farm. She writes fiction, creative nonfiction, and poetry. Her nonfiction has won such awards as the Emma Bell Miles Award for essay, the Wilma Dykeman Award and the Betty Grabehart Prize. Her work has appeared in *The Louisville Review, Kudzu, Now and Then, Literary Leo,* and *The Minnetonka Review*. She received her MFA in creative nonfiction from Spalding University.

Pauletta Hansel is the author of four poetry collections, including *The Lives We Live in Houses* and *What I Did There*. Her fifth, *Tangle,* is forthcoming from Wind Publications. She is co-editor of *Pine Mountain Sand & Gravel,* the literary publication of Southern Appalachian Writers Cooperative.

Hadley Hury's poetry and short fiction has appeared in *Appalachian Heritage, The James Dickey Review, Forge Journal, Image, Colorado Review, Green Mountains Review,* and numerous other journals, reviews, and magazines. He lives with his wife Marilyn in Louisville, Kentucky.

Andrew Jarvis is the author of *Choreography* (Johns Hopkins University), *Sound Points* (Red Bird Press), *Ascent* (Finishing Line Press), and *The Strait* (Homebound Publications). His poems have appeared or are forthcoming in *Valparaiso Poetry Review, Tulane Review, San Pedro River Review, Stonecoast Review,* and many other literary magazines. Jarvis holds an M.A. in Writing (Poetry) from Johns Hopkins University.

Loyal Jones is a writer, educator, and humorist, and one of the primary people responsible for the Appalachian Studies and Literature movement. A native of North Carolina, Loyal was the director of the Appalachian Center at Berea College from 1970 to 1993. Jones is the author of several highly influential books including *Appalachian Values* and *Faith and Meaning in the Southern Uplands.*

Dan Leach was born in Greenville, South Carolina, graduated from Clemson University in 2008, and taught in Charleston until 2014 when he relocated to Nebraska. He writes short fiction that explores connections between the South, masculinity, faith, and failure. His work has appeared in *New Madrid, Deep South Magazine, Two*

Bridges Review, Storm Cellar, Drafthorse, and elsewhere. He is currently at work on his first novel.

Donna J. Long is Professor of English and Editor of *Kestrel: A Journal of Literature and Art* at Fairmont State University in Fairmont, West Virginia. Her poems have appeared recently in *Kindred, Third Wednesday,* and *Cooweescoowee,* and have been anthologized in *The Southern Poetry Anthology, Vol. III* and *The Poets Guide to the Birds.*

Karen Salyer McElmurray's *Surrendered Child: A Birth Mother's Journey,* was an AWP Award Winner for Creative Nonfiction. Her novels are *The Motel of the Stars* and *Strange Birds in the Tree of Heaven.* Other stories and essays have appeared in *Iron Horse, Kenyon Review, Alaska Quarterly Review,* and *River Teeth,* and have been widely anthologized. She is a frequent visiting writer and lecturer at a variety of programs and reading series.

Amanda Jo Runyon is a mother, writer, and instructor in Pike County, Kentucky. Her fiction and poetry have appeared in journals such as *The Louisville Review, Still: The Journal, Pine Mountain Sand and Gravel,* and *Kudzu,* as well as *Seeking Its Own Level,* volume 4 of the *Motif* anthology series. She is co-editor of the literary journal *The Pikeville Review.*

C. Lynn Shaffer's chapbook *Life Spiral* was published by Finishing Line Press in 2014. Shaffer won the Morehead State University New Writers Award in 2006 for her poetry collection *Persistence of Vision,* which was published in 2008 by Wind Publications. Her poems have appeared in journals such as *Slant, Pisgah Review, Louisiana Literature, Mid-American Review, Wind, The Journal of Kentucky Studies,* and *The Heartland Review.*

Sean Stewart is a Brooklyn-based photographer originally from Pittsburgh, Pennsylvania. The purveyor of "socially informed art documentary photography," much of his work is set in western Pennsylvania and along I-80. Stewart's photographs have been featured in *VICE, Mossless,* and *Looking at Appalachia.*

Bradley R. Strahan taught poetry at Georgetown University for twelve years and has had six books of poetry and over 600 poems published. His 2011 book, *This Art of Losing,* has had critical praise and has been translated into French. His book of poems from a recent stay in Ireland was just released by BrickHouse Books.

Dean Marshall Tuck's stories have been featured in publications such as *EPOCH, The Los Angeles Review, Natural Bridge, Zone 3, Flash: The International Short-Short Story Magazine,* and others. He is an advisory editor for *Tar River Poetry* and an English instructor at Wayne Community College in Goldsboro, North Carolina.

A West Virginia native, **Jessie van Eerden** holds a B.A. in English from West Virginia University and an MFA in nonfiction writing from the University of Iowa. She is the author of the novel *Glorybound,* and her work has appeared in *The Oxford American, River Teeth, Image, Bellingham Review, Rock & Sling,* and other publications. She lives in West Virginia where she directs the low-residency MFA writing program of West Virginia Wesleyan College.

Doug Van Gundy teaches in the low-residency MFA program at West Virginia Wesleyan College, where he also directs the undergraduate Honors Program. His poems, essays and reviews have appeared in *The Oxford American, Poems & Plays, Ecotone, Fretboard Journal,* and *Poetry Salzburg Review.* He is also an award-winning fiddler and banjo player and performs as part of the old-time duo, Born Old.

Marianne Worthington is co-founder and poetry editor of *Still: The Journal.* She is author of the chapbook *Larger Bodies Than Mine,* winner of the 2007 Appalachian Book of the Year Award. Her work has appeared in *Grist, Shenandoah, Appalachian Heritage, 94 Creations, Pine Mountain Sand & Gravel, Kudzu,* and many other publications. She lives, writes, and teaches in southeastern Kentucky.